PASSION FOR COLOUR

PASSION FOR COLOUR

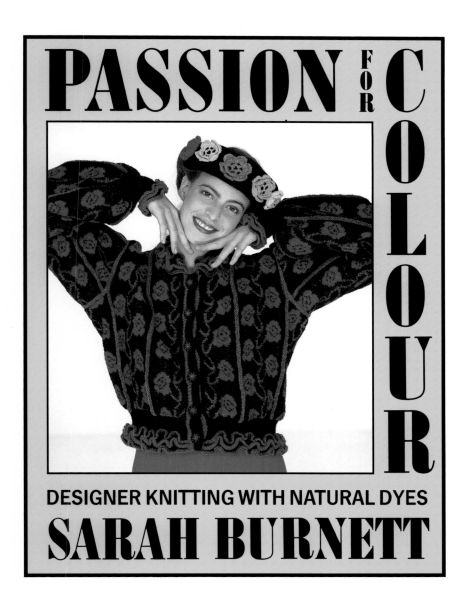

DESIGNER KNITTING WITH NATURAL DYES

SARAH BURNETT

Conran Octopus

First published in 1990 by
Conran Octopus Limited
37 Shelton Street
London WC2H 9HN

Project Editor   Cortina Butler
Art Editor   Karen Bowen
Copy Editor   Michelle Clark
Picture Research   Nadine Bazar
Production   Jackie Kernaghan
Editorial Assistant   Denise Bates
Special Photography   Anthony Crickmay, Jan Baldwin
Knitting Consultant   Maureen Briggs
Knitting Charts   Radius

Typeset by Flairplan
Printed and bound in Singapore by Toppan Printing Co.

British Library Cataloguing in Publication Data
Burnett, Sarah
    Passion for colour : designer knitting with natural dyes.
    I. Clothing. Knitting Designs
    I. Title
    646.4

ISBN 1-85029-244-2

CONTENTS

INTRODUCTION
8

COOKING WITH COLOUR

THE PATTERNS

GLOSSARY

STOCKISTS

ACKNOWLEDGMENTS

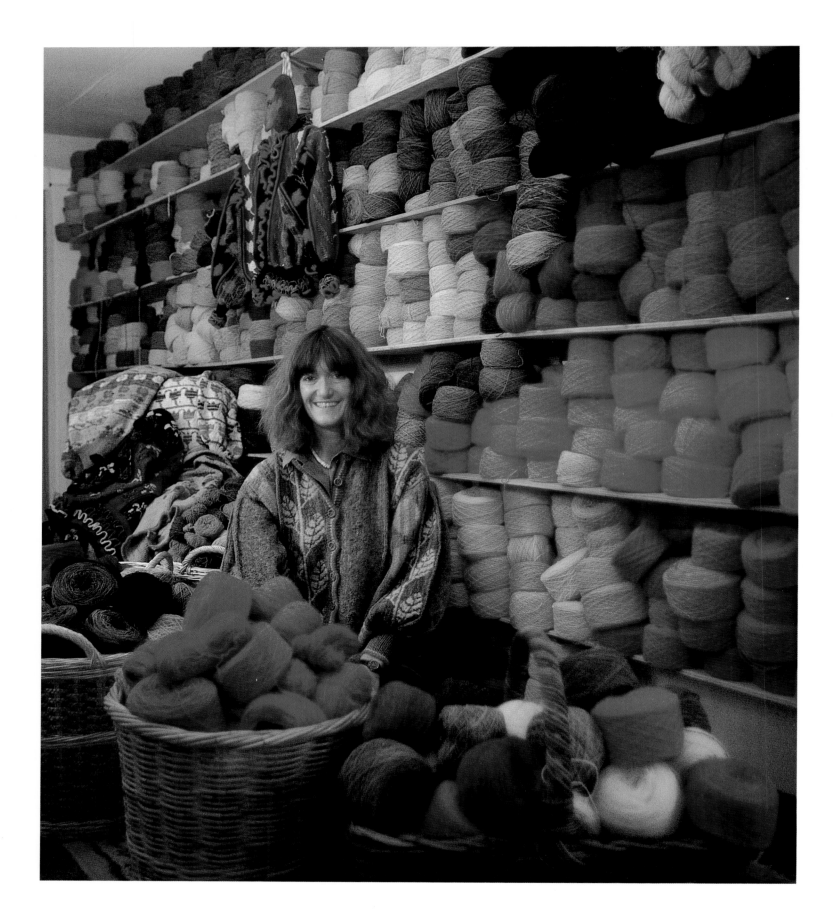

INTRODUCTION

Colourful clothes have always been my passion. As a teenager I dressed like a rainbow and my wardrobe remains a muddle of different textiles in every imaginable colour. Fabrics collected when travelling, or that I have bought or been given, fill every room in the house: Guatemalan weavings, quilted bedspreads, Turkish kelims, hand-rolled felt and embroidered silks and velvets. Even my old clothes have been given a new lease of life; the crêpe dresses I once eagerly hunted at jumble sales have ended their days as patchwork curtains, the leftovers from the curtains are now a multicoloured woven rag rug.

Travel and marriage and moving to the Dorset countryside changed my life considerably. Our small cottage looked out over water-meadows. I bought a potter's wheel and kiln and struggled in vain to make brightly coloured decorated pots. Our way of life was a classic period piece; my husband wrote novels, we kept sheep and chickens, grew vegetables, baked our own bread and made enough elderflower wine to entertain friends and last out the year.

The arrival of children meant making them winter jerseys. But the gaudy chemical colours of those first jerseys and hats made me long for something softer. I can no longer remember the first time I lowered a hank of wool into a saucepan of plant dye, but the results were a revelation. Outside, in the surrounding woods and meadows, lay the very colours I had been failing to find in my pottery. There was no holding back. Saucepans heaped with wool and enveloped in steam took over the kitchen and transformed the riches of the hedgerow into colours I had only ever seen in my dreams.

The more I experimented the more I was amazed by the depth and beauty of natural colour. Every other plant I gathered seemed capable of producing a new shade. But there were the inevitable disappointments, and I soon discovered that many plants gave muddy yellows, sludge browns and dirty greens. I planted a dye garden, hoping it would provide the bright blues and reds I was still searching for. For two years I waged war with the weeds, before finally accepting that the temperate English climate just wasn't capable of yielding the strong bright colours I wanted. Some of the best dye plants need sun and heat and it wasn't until I started using dyestuffs imported from South America and Africa that I knew I had found the answer.

Natural dyeing is thousands of years old, whereas chemical dyeing only dates to 1856 when William Perkin, an eighteen-year-old chemistry research assistant, accidentally discovered that an aniline dye could be produced from coal tar. He christened it 'mauve' and in 1857, with the help of his father and brother, set up a company in North London to manufacture the mauve dye. The chemical dye industry had been born.

Today, more than a century later, fabrics that don't run or fade come in every conceivable colour. Some are so garish that you can almost smell the chemicals that created them. In my opinion, the modern synthetic dye works make little attempt to achieve the endlessly subtle shades possible with natural dyes. You only have to look at an Elizabethan costume or a Baluchi rug to be aware of the gulf that divides plant from chemical dyes.

Natural dyes are not entirely without faults. Some of the colours fade a little and the nature of plants makes it difficult to dye the same shade consistently. But the quality of natural colours is unsurpassed and all the recipes I have included give magnificent

left Heaps of knitted sweaters, hanks of yarn and wool wound into balls and stacked on shelves are always present to fill the workshop with a mass of glorious pattern and colour.

overleaf Some of the most picturesque countryside in England lies in Dorset in the South West. Soft rolling hills grazed by sheep or showing the signs of habitation by Iron Age people lead down to the coast, which can be by turns idyllically peaceful or racked by violent storms.

colours that mellow and mature. The skill lies in turning their defects into virtues, two jerseys may share a pattern, even the same colours, but the variation in the dyeing gives each its uniqueness.

From the start I was determined to combine strong bright colours with extravagant designs and patterns. Just because a jersey is knitted from naturally dyed wool doesn't mean it has to be dull and lifeless. I also wanted my designs to be exciting to wear, even theatrical.

Many years ago I bought some Diaghilev ballet costumes at an auction. Serge Diaghilev was a Russian impresario whose introduction to the West of the Ballets Russes in 1909 transformed ballet and sparked off a revolution in fashion and design. Under him, dancers like Nijinsky and Pavlova danced to the music of Stravinsky wearing costumes designed by Bakst, Picasso, Matisse and Braque. The braided skirts and wool jackets with their dramatic full Russian sleeves that I bought that day were irresistible. I wore them constantly, and the sleeves of many of my own designs are a small tribute to their influence.

Many ideas have helped to shape my designs, but the knitting technique I use comes from a tiny windswept island in the North Atlantic on the same latitude as Greenland. Fair Isle is one of the most isolated of the Shetland Islands, but its impact on knitting has been immense and not just for the distinctive all-over pattern traditionally associated with it. Over the centuries the Islanders have evolved a method by which when one colour is in use the others are neatly woven into the back of the knitting. The result is as sturdy as the Islanders themselves, with the strength and texture of cloth.

Originally the Islanders used plant dyes, a tradition born out of necessity that sadly did not survive the arrival of synthetics. The marriage between natural dyes and Fair Isle techniques is a delight. Multitudes of different colours can be used. The body part of the jerseys is knitted in one piece and the sleeves are grafted on afterwards. There are no loose ends to unravel and the inside of the knitting is as perfect as the outside. The extra strength means the jerseys retain their shape and never deteriorate and the technique allows you to mingle in as many colours as you like, though without ever using more than three colours in a row.

The designs I have chosen for the book are the result of many years of experimentation. I am helped by being surrounded by a wonderfully cheerful team of knitters. We work closely together, improving and perfecting ideas, and they are the first to let me know if a design won't work.

I am often asked what inspired a particular design and I have tried to write a bit about each of the ones I have chosen for the book. Yet it hasn't always been easy. Some ideas stem from the colours obtained during the dyeing, but they might just as easily be sparked off by a flower or a scrap of colour and pattern in a painting.

What I have tried to do is create contemporary designs that are dramatic and easy to wear, but which still retain classical elegance and style. The combining of two traditional crafts makes the possibilities limitless. The dyeing is like cooking, and is surprisingly easy once a few basics are mastered. Natural dyes make everything you knit an individual creation that might one day become a family heirloom. It is also fun, and once you've made a start there will be no stopping!

The Fair Isle technique of weaving colours not in use into the back of the knitting means that garments knitted this way are as neat, and almost as beautiful, on the inside as on the outside.

COOKING WITH
COLOUR

GETTING STARTED

When I first started dyeing I used the plants growing round me in the English countryside. In this I was merely carrying on a tradition begun by primitive man, for natural dyeing is one of the earliest of all crafts. Dyes from shellfish, insects and plants were used for body decoration before the first textiles were woven, and the earliest fragments of weaving to survive still retain some of their original colour.

The Chinese dyed silk with indigo more than 5000 years ago, and by 1000 B.C. the ancient Phoenicians had perfected skills that changed little until the 19th century. It was they who first lowered themselves over cliffs to harvest a lichen called orchil which turned crimson and purple once steeped in stale urine.

By the Middle Ages, weld and dyer's broom were providing cloth mills with Lincoln green and Robin Hood and his men with clothing to match the colour of their forest refuge. Dyes that 'neither rain, wine, nor yet vinegar can stain' were in common use, and imported plants such as madder and indigo made fortunes for the merchants who traded in them.

My own attempts at gathering natural dyes were more modest. I grew woad (*Isatis tinctoria*) from seed, but otherwise made use of what was seasonally available, or could be dried and stored. Nettles gave dull greens. Elderberry dyes weren't fast – the wool lost colour in sunlight. But walnut husks, weld, onion skins and safflower all proved their worth and I still use them today.

Much of the pleasure came from experimenting with different plants and mordants – the metallic salts used to fix the colour. I soon learnt that the exact repetition of a precise colour was virtually impossible. Plants are dependent on their individual habitats, and weld grown on chalk gave a slightly richer yellow than that grown on clay. Annual variations in climate also had an effect, as did different conditions of storage and drying.

The dye recipes given in this book all employ readily obtainable dyestuffs, some of them imported and available from dye suppliers, others, such as onion skins, available in or around the home (see page 20). The wool used for dyeing must be unbleached – bleached wools resist dyes. All the patterns in this book have been designed for knitting in unplied Cheviot wool which has very little nap. The Magician's and Fair Isle sweaters have been knitted using two strands of wool. See Stockists (page 158) for suppliers and alternative wools.

EQUIPMENT FOR MORDANTING AND DYEING

1 Weighing scales
2 Rubber gloves
3 5 litre (8 pint) stainless steel saucepan used for mordanting and dyeing only
4 One 500 ml (1 pint) heatproof glass measuring jug
5 Muslin or nylon bag for tyeing up dyestuffs
6 Stick for stirring
7 Teaspoon
8 Olive oil soap (or other natural soap)
9 115 g (4 oz) hanks of wool

See page 30 for key to equipment for indigo dyeing

MORDANTING

Mordanting always precedes dyeing. It is the method by which a mordant – one of a range of metallic salts – is used to make the colour fast. Without it, natural dyeing would be impossible, and, apart from indigo dyeing which is a process unlike any other, there is only one dye recipe in this book that doesn't require a mordant. Different mordants give different colours from the same dyestuff, thus, by varying the mordant, cochineal can produce either red, pink or purple.

   The process is very simple and certainly more scientific than in the past, when such things as wood ash, copper filings and bran were used. One tale even tells of a dead cat being thrown into a vat by a dyer desperate to get the colour he wanted!

MORDANTS

All mordants must be clearly labelled 'Poisonous' and stored in a safe dry place out of reach of children. Take them out only when you are ready to use them and put them away again as soon as you have measured out what you need. See Stockists (page 158) for names and addresses of suppliers of mordants.

ALUM
potassium aluminium sulphate
This is traditionally the most important of all the ancient mordants and was used with madder as early as 2000 B.C. Using too much alum makes the wool sticky. Alum is now supplied as a white powder.

COPPER SULPHATE
This is often known as 'blue copperas' and is the most common of the copper mordants. The blue crystals are poisonous and should always be handled with particular care.

CHROME
potassium dichromate, bichromate of potash
This metal was introduced in about 1800 and is widely used with red dyes. The orange crystals are sensitive to light: store them in a dark place.

TIN
stannous chloride
Tin is always used in very small quantities and should be rinsed out thoroughly after mordanting as it makes wool brittle, but it is superb for brightening reds. It is supplied as white crystals.

OXALIC ACID
This is corrosive and so needs to be handled with special care – always wear gloves. Natural oxalic acid is found in garden sorrel and rhubarb stalks. It is supplied commercially as a white powder.

ACETIC ACID
or vinegar
This is used in small quantities to help the wool absorb the mordant.

CREAM OF TARTAR
tartaric acid
This helps to soften the wool when harsh mordants are used. It is supplied as a white powder and is also used in baking.

MORDANTING METHOD

The method is the same for all the mordants used in this book. Follow the recipes given on pages 24–28 for quantities.

1 Tie a 115 g (4 oz) hank of unbleached wool with a loose figure of eight. Tie it in four places to stop tangling.

2 Wash and wet the wool thoroughly.

3 Measure the mordant into the heatproof glass measuring jug. Add 140 ml (¼ pint) of warm water and stir until dissolved.

4 Put 2¼ litres (4 pints) of warm water into the saucepan, place on medium heat and add the mordant mixture. Stir.

5 Put the wetted wool into the saucepan and stir. Simmer gently for 30 minutes.

6 Remove the wool and throw away the water in the saucepan. Wash out the saucepan ready for dyeing.

7 Gently squeeze excess water from the wool and then keep it wet (in a plastic bag if necessary) ready for dyeing.

NATURAL DYESTUFFS

The dyestuffs listed on this page are all available from dye suppliers or found in the home. But all plants or berries which stain can probably be employed in natural dyeing, and you can be sure of results using those which include the Latin name *tinctoria*, meaning 'to stain'. Leave all rare flowers well alone, but otherwise don't be afraid of experimenting with common local plants. Simply pick twice the weight of plant stuff to that of the wool you want to dye, having first mordanted the wool with an alum mordant (see pages 18–19). Boil the plant in twice its volume of water until the water changes colour, add the wool and simmer until the wool has coloured. Wash the wool and dry it. Try to record the plants used, the time of year they were picked and keep samples of the dyed wool for reference.

1 BRAZILWOOD
Caesalpinia braziliensis
Described in the 18th century as giving the colour of 'claret wine', these dark wood chippings dye a range of reds, browns and burgundies. The dye is at its most concentrated in the heartwood. Other trees in the family include peachwood and **REDWOOD**. Before the discovery of the Americas most brazilwood came from India, but so much was found growing in part of South America that it gave its name to a country – Brazil.

2 COCHINEAL
Coccus cacti

> 'Painted for sight and essenced for the smell
> Like a frigate fraught with spice and cochineal,
> Sail in the ladies.'

So wrote Alexander Pope, noting cochineal's role as a colour dye in cosmetics. It is obtained from a dried insect that lives on the prickly pear cactus and provides the most brilliant reds and pinks, including Huntsman's scarlet. The cacti are grown as a crop in Central America, the West Indies and the Canary Islands, and the insects are brushed off at harvest time.

3 FUSTIC
Chlorophora tinctoria
These yellow chippings come from the dyer's mulberry tree, or Cuba fustic, which grows in the West Indies and Mexico. The dye it produces is extremely fast, and, combined with other plants, it was used to dye khaki before the invention of a suitable synthetic. I get vibrant yellows and golds, and a glorious green when 'top dyed' with indigo.

4 INDIGO
Indigofera tinctoria
Historically the most famous of all dyes, this blue powder is extracted from the leaves of *Indigofera*, a plant genus grown widely throughout the tropics. The leaves are fermented, and the sediment dried and ground to prepare it for dyeing. Its blues are outstanding, and it is still widely used in India. The analysis of natural indigo followed by its synthetic manufacture in 1897 led directly to the evolution of blue denim.

5 LOGWOOD
Haemotoxylin campechianum
I use logwood chips for deep navy blues and soft greys. The trees grow widely in Mexico and the Caribbean, where the yellow timber turns brown as soon as it is felled. It is another dye of historical importance, mainly because there was no equivalent in the Old World and it is the only plant dye to give a true black on wool.

6 MADDER
Rubia tinctorum
This is a dye renowned for its reds and extracted from the root of an herbaceous plant which grows widely throughout Europe and the Middle East, especially France and Turkey. The medieval papal court owed the scarlet robes of its cardinals to madder, but there are fragments dyed with it which date back to at least 3000 B.C. Old roots have the richest concentration of colour, and the plant grows best on chalk. It can be grown domestically but the root is also commercially supplied (chopped) and I use it for a range of beautiful dusty pinks.

7 ONIONS

Allium cepa

Yellow onion skins are undoubtedly the most common and easiest of all dyestuffs, and they give me wonderful rusts and pale browns. Just peel off the outer dry skin whenever you need an onion for cooking and store the skins in a paper bag until needed. Red onion skins will give a different shade of yellow.

8 WALNUT HUSKS/9 LEAVES

Juglans regia, Juglans nigra

This is the only dye I don't combine with a mordant, although when mordanted with alum the dried leaves do give various shades of brown. It is a 'substantive' dye which does not require a mordant to make it fast. I collect the fallen shells and husks from the tree, storing them in a jar of water in a dark cupboard until needed. However, they are supplied as chopped chips, so don't despair if a tree doesn't grow nearby.

10 WELD

Reseda luteola

This tall elegant biennial plant is my favourite dye plant, and is easily grown. It is also known as wild mignonette or dyer's rocket, and for centuries its bright yellows have been used for dyeing. There is little variation in results between the fresh and the dried plant, but hang it upside down in bundles if you want to store it.

See Stockists (page 158) for suppliers of natural dyestuffs.

DYEING

Before you start dyeing there are a few points to bear in mind. Do not expect the wool to be an even colour when dyed, it may be patchy – mine always is – this is part of the charm of naturally dyed wool. Moreover, all dyestuffs will give a slightly different colour each time they are used. Natural dyes are not uniform. Experiment a little with the dyes – use these recipes as foundations on which to build.

   Be careful when using dyestuffs. Always wear rubber gloves and keep children out of the way where possible. The dyestuffs are no more poisonous than ordinary household cleaners but exercise the same amount of care with their storage and use. Always wash the wool carefully to stop it from tangling and felting.

   Enjoy using natural dyes and have fun. Don't worry if you get entirely the wrong colour. Use your imagination and change the colours intended for the design: it always works. I try to design all of my sweaters to make the best use of naturally dyed colours, thus colours which would clash if chemically dyed merge and mix as a harmonious whole. The colours may be bright, but they are never gaudy.

METHOD FOR DYEING

This method of dyeing applies to all the recipes in this book except for indigo (see pages 30–31). However, there are slight variations so follow the specific instructions for individual colours on the following pages.

1 Put 2¼ litres (4 pints) of water into the stainless steel saucepan.

2 Add the dyestuff according to the recipe. Stir.

3 Put the mordanted wool (see pages 18–19) into the saucepan and simmer for the length of time given in the recipe. Do not stir the wool; turn it over once.

4 Remove the pan from the heat and allow the wool to cool in the pan.

5 Remove the dyed wool and wash well with warm water and olive oil soap or other natural soap. Handle the wool very gently to avoid tangling and felting.

6 Rinse the wool until the water runs clear.

7 Hang the wool out on a washing line to dry.

centre left *Finely ground cochineal, logwood chips tied in a muslin bag and onion skins have been added to pans of water (step* **2***).* **main picture left** *Simmering in the dyes (step* **3***) transforms natural coloured wool into brilliant shades of crimson, navy and buttercup yellow.* **above** *After the wool has been dyed it is washed with warm water and soap and then thoroughly rinsed (step* **6***).*

REDS

CRIMSON

Mordant   1 teaspoon cream of tartar
              ½ teaspoon tin
Dyestuff 28 g (1 oz) cochineal, finely ground
Wool   115 g (4 oz) hank of natural yarn

See pages 18–19 for mordanting instructions.

Mix the cochineal to a smooth paste with a little warm water in a stainless steel saucepan. Add 2¼ litres (4 pints) of cold water to the paste. Stir well.

Put the mordanted wool into the saucepan and place over a very low heat. Bring to the boil very slowly and gently simmer for 20 minutes. Remove from the heat and allow the wool to cool in the pan.

Remove the dyed wool and wash well with warm water and olive oil soap or other natural soap. Rinse the wool until the water runs clear and then hang out to dry.

SCARLET

Mordant   ½ teaspoon oxalic acid
              ½ teaspoon tin
              1 teaspoon cream of tartar
Dyestuff 28 g (1 oz) cochineal, finely ground
Wool   115 g (4 oz) hank of natural yarn

Method as for Crimson

RED

Mordant   28 g (1 oz) alum
Dyestuff 170 g (6 oz) brazilwood, tied in a muslin bag
Wool   115 g (4 oz) hank of natural yarn

See pages 18–19 for mordanting instructions.

Put the bag of brazilwood into a stainless steel saucepan with 2¾ litres (5 pints) of water and boil for 1 hour. Remove the bag of brazilwood.

Put the mordanted wool into the saucepan and simmer for 30 minutes. Remove from the heat and allow the wool to cool in the pan.

Remove the dyed wool and wash well with warm water and olive oil soap or other natural soap. Rinse the wool until the water runs clear and then hang out to dry.

PINKS

MAGENTA

Mordant   28 g (1 oz) alum
Dyestuff 28 g (1 oz) cochineal, finely ground
Wool   115 g (4 oz) hank of natural yarn

See pages 18–19 for mordanting instructions.

Mix the cochineal to a smooth paste with a little warm water in a stainless steel saucepan. Add 2¼ litres (4 pints) of cold water to the paste. Stir well.

Put the mordanted wool into the saucepan and place over a very low heat. Bring to the boil very slowly and gently simmer for 20 minutes. Remove from the heat and allow the wool to cool in the pan.

Remove the dyed wool, wash well, rinse and then hang out to dry.

PINK

Mordant   28 g (1 oz) alum
Dyestuff 1 teaspoon cochineal, finely ground
Wool   115 g (4 oz) hank of natural yarn

Method as for Magenta

PALE PINK

Mordant   28 g (1 oz) alum
Dyestuff ½ teaspoon cochineal, finely ground
Wool   115 g (4 oz) hank of natural yarn

Method as for Magenta

REDWOOD PINK

Mordant   28 g (1 oz) alum
Dyestuff 85 g (3 oz) redwood, tied in a muslin bag
Wool   115 g (4 oz) hank of natural yarn

See pages 18–19 for mordanting instructions.

Put the bag of redwood into a stainless steel saucepan with 2¾ litres (5 pints) of water and boil for 1 hour. Remove the bag of redwood.

Put the mordanted wool into the saucepan and simmer for 30 minutes. Remove from the heat and allow the wool to cool in the pan.

Remove the dyed wool, wash well, rinse and then hang out to dry.

1   crimson
2   scarlet
3   red

1   magenta
2   pink
3   pale pink
4   redwood pink

WINES

ELDERBERRY

Mordant ½ teaspoon chrome
Dyestuff 85 g (3 oz) brazilwood, tied in a muslin bag
Wool 115 g (4 oz) hank of natural yarn

See pages 18–19 for mordanting instructions.

Put the bag of brazilwood into a stainless steel saucepan with 2¾ litres (5 pints) of water and boil for 1 hour. Remove the dyestuff.

Put the mordanted wool into the saucepan and simmer for 30 minutes. Remove from the heat and allow the wool to cool in the pan.

Remove the dyed wool, wash well, rinse and then hang out to dry.

LIGHT ELDERBERRY

Mordant ½ teaspoon chrome
Dyestuff 28 g (1 oz) brazilwood, tied in a muslin bag
Wool 115 g (4 oz) hank of natural yarn

Method as for Elderberry

GRAPE

Mordant ½ teaspoon chrome
Dyestuff 28 g (1 oz) cochineal, finely ground
Wool 115 g (4 oz) hank of natural yarn

Method as for Crimson.

BURGUNDY

Mordant ½ teaspoon copper sulphate
          ½ teaspoon acetic acid
Dyestuff 170 g (6 oz) brazilwood, tied in a muslin bag
Wool 115 g (4 oz) hank of natural yarn

Method as for Elderberry

MADDER

Mordant ½ teaspoon chrome
Dyestuff 115 g (4 oz) madder chips, tied in a muslin bag
Wool 115 g (4 oz) hank of natural yarn

See pages 18–19 for mordanting instructions.

Put the bag of madder chips into a stainless steel saucepan with 2¾ litres (5 pints) of cold water. Stir well.

Put the mordanted wool into the saucepan. Bring to simmering point very slowly and gently simmer for 20 minutes. Do not boil. Remove from the heat and allow to cool in the pan.

Remove the dyed wool, wash well, rinse and then hang out to dry.

NAVY AND GREYS

NAVY

Mordant ½ teaspoon copper sulphate
Dyestuff 57 g (2 oz) logwood, tied in a muslin bag
Wool 115 g (4 oz) hank of natural yarn

See pages 18–19 for mordanting instructions.

Put the bag of logwood into a stainless steel saucepan with 2¾ litres (5 pints) of water and boil for 45 minutes. Remove the bag of logwood.

Put the mordanted wool into the saucepan and simmer for 20 minutes. Remove from the heat and allow to cool in the pan.

Remove the dyed wool and then wash well with warm water and olive oil soap or other natural soap. Rinse the wool until the water runs clear then hang out to dry.

DARK GREY

Mordant ½ teaspoon chrome
Dyestuff 14 g (½ oz) logwood, tied in a muslin bag
Wool 115 g (4 oz) hank of natural yarn

Method as for Navy

GREY

Mordant ½ teaspoon chrome
Dyestuff 1 teaspoon logwood
Wool 115 g (4 oz) hank of natural yarn

Method as for Navy

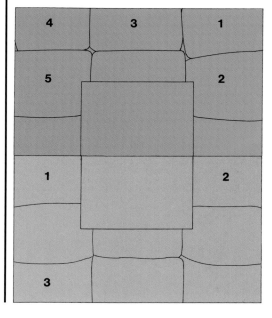

1 elderberry
2 light elderberry
3 grape
4 burgundy
5 madder

1 navy
2 dark grey
3 grey

YELLOWS

BUTTERCUP YELLOW

Mordant   28 g (1 oz) alum
Dyestuff 28 g (1 oz) onion skins
Wool   115 g (4 oz) hank of natural yarn

See pages 18–19 for mordanting instructions.
   Put the onion skins into a stainless steel saucepan with 2¼ litres (4 pints) of water and simmer for 30 minutes.
   Put the mordanted wool into the saucepan and simmer for a good 20 minutes. Remove from the heat and allow the wool to cool in the pan.
   Remove the dyed wool and wash well with warm water and olive oil soap or other natural soap. Rinse well, then hang out to dry.

YELLOW

Mordant   28 g (1 oz) alum
Dyestuff 85 g (3 oz) weld, chopped
Wool   115 g (4 oz) hank of natural yarn

See pages 18–19 for mordanting instructions.
   Put the weld into a stainless steel saucepan with 2¼ litres (4 pints) of water and boil for 30 minutes.
   Put the mordanted wool into the saucepan and simmer for a good 20 minutes. Remove from the heat and allow the wool to cool in the pan.
   Remove the dyed wool and wash well with warm water and olive oil soap or other natural soap. Rinse well, then hang out to dry.

PRIMROSE

Mordant   28 g (1 oz) alum
Dyestuff 1 teaspoon fustic chips, tied in a muslin bag
Wool   115 g (4 oz) hank of natural yarn

See pages 18–19 for mordanting instructions.
   Put the bag of fustic into a stainless steel saucepan with 2¼ litres (4 pints) of water and boil for 40 minutes.
   Put the mordanted wool into the saucepan and stir. Simmer for 20 minutes. Remove from the heat and allow the wool to cool in the pan.
   Remove the dyed wool and wash well with warm water and olive oil soap or other natural soap. Rinse well, then hang out to dry.

OCHRE AND WALNUTS

OCHRE

Mordant   ½ teaspoon chrome
Dyestuff 28 g (1 oz) onion skins
Wool   115 g (4 oz) hank of natural yarn

See pages 18–19 for mordanting instructions.
   Put the onion skins into a stainless steel saucepan with 2¼ litres (4 pints) of water and simmer for 30 minutes.
   Put the mordanted wool into the saucepan and simmer for 30 minutes. Remove from the heat and allow the wool to cool in the pan.
   Remove the dyed wool and wash well with warm water and olive oil soap or other natural soap. Rinse the wool and then hang out to dry.

WALNUT

Mordant   28 g (1 oz) alum
Dyestuff 28 g (1 oz) walnut husks
Wool   115 g (4 oz) hank of natural yarn

See pages 18–19 for mordanting instructions.
   Put the walnut husks into a stainless steel saucepan with 2¼ litres (4 pints) of water and simmer for 40 minutes.
   Put the mordanted wool into the saucepan and simmer for 40 minutes. Remove from the heat and allow the wool to cool in the pan.
   Remove the dyed wool and wash well with warm water and olive oil soap or other natural soap. Rinse the wool and then hang out to dry.

PALE WALNUT

No mordant
Dyestuff 28 g (1 oz) walnut leaves
Wool   115 g (4 oz) hank of natural yarn

Put the walnut leaves into a stainless steel saucepan with 2¼ litres (4 pints) of water and simmer for 40 minutes.
   Wet thoroughly the hank of *unmordanted* wool. Put the wool into the saucepan and simmer for 30 minutes. Remove from the heat and allow the wool to cool in the pan.
   Remove the dyed wool and wash well with warm water and olive oil soap or other natural soap. Rinse the wool and then hang out to dry.

1   buttercup yellow
2   yellow
3   primrose

1   ochre
2   walnut
3   pale walnut

INDIGO DYEING

Indigo dyeing is unlike any other dyeing process. Because the blue powder is not easily soluble in water, a stock solution is prepared. The powder is mixed into a smooth paste with a solution of caustic soda and then the oxygen in the mixture is eliminated by adding a solution of sodium dithionite (see Stockists, page 158) which turns the paste into a greenish-yellow liquid. The wool is immersed in a dye bath made with the stock solution, and finally oxidizes as it comes out, so changing from yellow to blue. The process is quite straightforward. Be very careful as some of the ingredients are toxic and indigo easily stains. Keep the bucket or saucepan for indigo dyeing only.

EQUIPMENT

1 Weighing scales
2 Pestle and mortar
3 Rubber gloves
4 Water thermometer
5 5 litre (8 pint) stainless steel bucket (or saucepan)
6 Two 500 ml (1 pint) heatproof glass measuring jugs
7 Teaspoon
8 Dessertspoon
9 Household saucepan
10 Stick for stirring
11 1 litre (2 pint) glass jar
12 Olive oil soap (or other natural soap)
13 115 g (4 oz) hanks of wool

METHOD FOR INDIGO DYEING

Preparing Indigo Stock Solution

28 g (1 oz) natural powdered indigo
42 g (1 ½ oz) caustic soda
28 g (1 oz) sodium dithionite

1 Put the indigo powder into a mortar and grind to a smooth, creamy paste with a little warm water and a pestle.

2 Measure 280 ml (½ pint) of warm water into a heatproof glass measuring jug and add the caustic soda. Stir until dissolved.

3 Measure 280 ml (½ pint) of warm water into another heatproof glass measuring jug and add the sodium dithionite, stirring *very gently* to dissolve it.

4 Pour the indigo paste into a large, 1 litre (2 pint) jar. Rinse the pestle with a little more water over the jar in order not to waste any indigo.

5 Add the solution of caustic soda to the jam jar.

6 Add the solution of sodium dithionite carefully to the jam jar, trying not to create any air bubbles. Stir very gently.

7 Stand the jam jar in a pan of very hot water. Keep checking that the temperature of the liquid in the jar does not exceed 60°C (140°F). Let this stand for 30–60 minutes until the liquid in the jar is a murky yellow/green. The indigo stock solution is now ready for use and can be stored for up to 6 weeks.

Preparing an Indigo Dye Bath

8   Fill a special stainless steel bucket or saucepan with 2¾ litres (5 pints) of warm water.

9   Sprinkle one teaspoon of sodium dithionite onto the warm water to reduce the oxygen.

10 Heat the water very gently. The temperature should be somewhere between 50° and 60°C (120° and 140°F). The water should never exceed 60°C (140°F) – overheating is disastrous and turns the wool brown.

Completing Indigo Dyeing

11 Prepare the dye bath as above.

12 Thoroughly wet the wool.

13 Measure out the Indigo Stock Solution according to the recipe for the shade of indigo that you require (see over) and add very carefully to the dye bath. Stir extremely gently.

14 Put on rubber gloves and dip the wetted wool into the bath for the number of seconds specified in the recipe, squeezing it gently under water to make sure that the indigo is absorbed. Lift the wool *gently* out of the bath and watch it turn from yellow to greenish blue in the air.

15 Dip the wool again according to the recipe and watch the colour change when you lift it out.

16 Hang the wool out on a washing line for 30 minutes to oxidize again.

17 Wash the wool very thoroughly with warm water and olive oil soap or other natural soap. Rinse it until the water runs clear and then hang it out to dry.

Greens are created by first dyeing wool yellow then dyeing it for a second time in an indigo dye bath. The wool changes colour from yellow to green as it emerges into the air and oxidizes.

INDIGO BLUES

DARK INDIGO BLUE

6 dessertspoons Indigo Stock Solution (page 30)
115 g (4 oz) hank of natural yarn

Prepare an indigo dye bath (see page 30).

Thoroughly wet the wool. Measure out the stock solution and add very carefully to the dye bath. Stir extremely gently.

Put on rubber gloves and dip the wetted wool into the bath for 60 seconds (count to 60), squeezing it gently under water to make sure that the indigo is absorbed. Lift the wool gently out of the bath and watch it turn from yellow to greenish blue in the air. Dip the wool for another 60 seconds and watch it turn a darker blue when you lift it out again.

Hang the wool out on a washing line for 30 minutes then wash it very thoroughly with warm water and olive oil soap or other natural soap. Rinse the wool until the water runs clear and then hang it out to dry.

MEDIUM INDIGO BLUE

3 dessertspoons Indigo Stock Solution (page 30)
115 g (4 oz) hank of natural yarn

Prepare the dye bath and follow the method for Dark Indigo Blue, but dip the wool *three* times for only 10 seconds each time.

PALE INDIGO BLUE

1 dessertspoon Indigo Stock Solution (page 30)
115 g (4 oz) hank of natural yarn

Prepare the dye bath and follow the method for Dark Indigo Blue but dip the wool *once* only for 10 seconds.

GREENS

The most exquisite greens are produced by 'top dyeing' wool that has first been dyed yellow in an indigo bath.

GRASS GREEN

Yellow dye
Mordant   28 g (1 oz) alum
Dyestuff   85 g (3 oz) weld
Top dye   3 dessertspoons Indigo Stock Solution (page 30)
Wool   115 g (4 oz) hank of natural yarn

See pages 18–19 for mordanting instructions then follow procedure for Yellow page 28.

Top dye the wool following the procedure for Medium Indigo Blue.

OLIVE GREEN

Yellow dye
Mordant   28 g (1 oz) alum
Dyestuff   57 g (2 oz) fustic chips, tied in a muslin bag
Top dye   3 dessertspoons Indigo Stock Solution (page 30)
Wool   115 g (4 oz) hank of natural yarn

See pages 18–19 for mordanting instructions then follow procedure for Primrose page 28.

Top dye the wool following the procedure for Medium Indigo Blue.

BLUE GREEN

Yellow dye
Mordant   28 g (1 oz) alum
Dyestuff   28 g (1 oz) weld
Top dye   6 dessertspoons Indigo Stock Solution (page 30)
Wool   115 g (4 oz) hank of natural yarn

See pages 18–19 for mordanting instructions then follow procedure for Yellow page 28.

Top dye the wool following the procedure for Dark Indigo Blue.

1   dark indigo blue
2   medium indigo
    blue
3   pale indigo blue

1   grass green
2   olive green
3   blue green

THE
PATTERNS

● The **Glossary of Knitting Terms and Techniques** (page 154) contains tips and information which will help you greatly in knitting the garments, so read it **before** you start to knit.

● All the garments are designed to be knitted in unplied Cheviot wool unless otherwise stated in the **Materials** section.

● It is essential to knit a tension square before you start the pattern, changing the needle size if necessary to obtain the tension required.

● In general, the pattern charts are coloured to correspond to the garments in the photographs. However, natural dyeing does not produce a consistent strength of colour and the garments are designed to make the most of this varied effect. Where a random effect is intended, the charts are also coloured randomly. There are no rigid rules and it is open to you to use the colours in the creative combination of your choice.

● When working from the charts, begin at stitch 1, row 1 unless otherwise stated. Follow the chart, repeating as necessary, to the end of the row. Rows will not always begin and end with a complete pattern repeat, therefore when working subsequent rows be sure to start with the stitch immediately above the last stitch worked on the chart.

● Under the **Materials** listed for each pattern, a pair of needles is usually given for the main part of the knitting. When large numbers of stitches are being worked, you can substitute a long circular needle and work in rows.

● The garments should be washed carefully by hand with a neutral washing agent in lukewarm water. You should always spin the water out of them in a washing machine to prevent them from losing their shape, but do not spin dry.

● Abbreviations used in the patterns:

beg	beginning
ch st	chain stitch
cont	continue
dec	decrease
d m st	double moss stitch
inc	increase
k	knit
k2 tog	knit 2 stitches together
m st	moss stitch
p	purl
patt	pattern
rem	remaining
rep	repeat
rev st st	reverse stocking stitch
sl st	slip st
st st	stocking stitch
tog	together

ADULT FAIR ISLE

The first jerseys I knitted up using natural dyes were Fair Isle. They were robust, light, and the colours suited the all-over patterning. Mine differ from the traditional design because each time the patterning is repeated the colour combinations change. The thicker yarn and tapering sleeves make this one quicker to knit. I have deliberately avoided giving specific instructions as to how the colours should be put together as naturally dyed colours never clash, and it's fun trying different combinations. Simply change colours every time you complete the patterning on the graph.

MATERIALS
Circular 2¼ mm (size 13) needle 80 cm (31½ in) long
Set of 4 double-pointed 2¼ mm (size 13) needles
Circular 4 mm (size 8) needles 40 cm (16 in) and 80 cm (31½ in) long
Pair of 4 mm (size 8) needles
7 stitch holders

WEIGHT OF YARN AND COLOURS
Plied yarn
17 colours in 57 g (2 oz) balls
170 g (6 oz) in one colour (A) for ribs
(Instead of plied yarn you can use 2 strands of ordinary yarn, knitted together.)

MEASUREMENTS
Length from top of shoulder to bottom edge of sweater: 76 cm (30 in)
Actual width all round at underarm: 122 cm (48 in)
Sleeve length: 58.5 cm (23 in)

TENSION
Over pattern, using 4 mm (size 8) needles, 23 stitches and 25 rows to 10 cm (4 in).

IMPORTANT
● The colours you use for this pattern are entirely up to you, so each sweater will be unique. Use as many

Top of garment

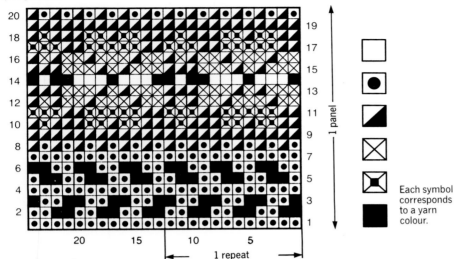

Bottom of garment

Odd-numbered rows are knit, worked from right to left.

Even-numbered rows are purl, worked from left to right.

Each symbol corresponds to a yarn colour.

brightly coloured wool around the first stitch each time you begin a round so that you can find the beginning.
● The sleeves are knitted on a circular needle and worked from shoulder to cuff, so remember to reverse the order of the pattern, that is, you work from row 20 to row 1.

INSTRUCTIONS
FRONT AND BACK

With 2¼ mm (size 13) circular needle and A, cast on 240 sts.
Work 24 rounds in k1 p1 rib.
Inc round *k4, inc into next st: rep from * to end (288 sts).
Change to 4 mm (size 8) 80 cm (31½ in) long circular needle and work rounds 1–20 of chart 5 times (100 rounds).

Divide for front and back
Slip 1st 14 sts onto a st holder (holder 1) for underarm then patt 116 sts. Leave rem sts on circular needle and, with pair of 4 mm (size 8) needles, work straight on these 116 sts until 3 complete panels and 1 row have been worked.
Row 2 (wrong side facing) patt 39 sts, turn.
Row 3 k2 tog, patt to end.
Row 4 patt 38 sts, turn.
Row 5 k2 tog, patt to end (37 sts).
Rows 6 and 7 as chart, then slip these 37 sts onto a st holder for left back shoulder. With wrong side facing slip next 38 sts onto a st holder for back neck. Cont on rem 39 sts as follows:
Row 2 (wrong side facing) patt to end.
Row 3 patt to last 2 sts, k2 tog, turn.
Row 4 patt, turn.
Row 5 patt to last 2 sts, k2 tog, turn (37 sts).
Rows 6 and 7 as chart, then slip these 37 sts onto a st holder for right back shoulder. With right side facing slip next 28 sts onto a st holder for left underarm (holder 2). Patt 116 sts and slip rem 14 sts onto holder 1. With 4 mm (size 8) needles, work 2 complete panels and 4 rows on these 116 sts.
Row 5 patt 43 sts, turn.
Row 6 cast off 2 sts, patt to end.
Row 7 as chart.
Row 8 cast off 2 sts, patt to end.
Row 9 as chart.
Row 10 cast off 1 st, patt to end.
Row 11 as chart.
Row 12 cast off 1 st, patt to end (37 sts).
Work straight until row 7 of next panel has been worked, then slip sts onto a st holder for left front shoulder. Slip next 30 sts onto a st holder for front neck and then work rem 43 sts (right side facing) as follows:
Row 5 cast off 2 sts, patt to end.
Row 6 as chart.
Row 7 cast off 2 sts, patt to end.
Row 8 as chart.
Row 9 cast off 1 st, patt to end.

colours as you wish but make sure that every panel has a different colour sequence.
● When working front and back the 'dots' on row 20 of panel should be worked in the same colour as the 'dots' on rows 1–8 of following pattern, as they are part of same colour stripe.
● When working st st using just one colour twist a spare ball of the same colour yarn across the back of

work to keep the thickness of the garment even.
● The sweater is knitted on a circular needle as far as the underarm, so every round of the chart up to that point is knit.
● When using the circular needles, take great care on the first round to ensure that the stitches are not twisted around the needle.
● When knitting in the round, loop a short strand of

Row 10 as chart.
Row 11 cast off 1 st, patt to end (37 sts).
Work straight until work matches left side of neck. Leave sts on a spare needle for right front shoulder.

Shoulder seams

Block (see page 155) garment and press carefully on wrong side using a damp cloth. With right sides together graft (see page 155) right front shoulder to right back shoulder and left front shoulder to left back shoulder. Weave in any loose ends using a darning needle (do not just cut them off).

SLEEVES

Remember to k all rounds and panels in rev order – from row 20–1.

With right side facing and 4 mm (size 8) 40 cm (16 in) long circular needle, slip last 14 sts from holder 1 onto left needle and k them using 1st colour you used for 6th panel of front and back. Then pick up and k 58 sts up to shoulder seam, 58 sts down to st holder and then k the 14 sts left on holder (144 sts). Then, using 1st 2 colours you used for 6th panel of front and back, work chart in rev order, rounds 8–2.
Round 1 *k10, k2 tog; rep from * to end (132 sts).
Rounds 20–2 use same colours as 5th panel of front and back.
Round 1 *k9, k2 tog; rep from * to end (120 sts).
Rounds 20–2 use same colours as 4th panel of front and back.
Round 1 *k8, k2 tog; rep from * to end (108 sts).
Rounds 20–2 use same colours as 3rd panel of front and back.
Round 1 *k7, k2 tog; rep from * to end (96 sts).
Rounds 20–2 use same colours as 2nd panel of front and back.
Round 1 *k6, k2 tog; rep from * to end (84 sts).
Rounds 20–1 use same colours as 1st panel of front and back, then change to set of 4 double-pointed 2¼ mm (size 13) needles and join on A.
Next round *k2 tog, k2; rep from * to last 4 sts, k2 tog, k2 tog (62 sts). Then work 30 rounds in k1 p1 rib. Cast off loosely in rib.

NECKBAND

With right side facing and 2¼ mm (size 13) double-pointed needles and A, k the 38 sts for back of neck, pick up and k 27 sts along left side of neck, k the 30 sts for front of neck and pick up and k 27 sts along right side of neck (122 sts). Work 9 rounds in k1 p1 rib.
Next round p (to make foldline). Work 9 more rounds in k1 p1 rib, then cast off loosely in rib. Fold band to inside along foldline and stitch down neatly.

FINISHING

Weave in any loose ends using a darning needle (do not just cut them off). Block (see page 155) garment and press carefully using a damp cloth, but do not press ribbing.

CHILD'S FAIR ISLE

Cardigans like this one were the first I ever made for my children when they were small. Baking bread, growing vegetables, keeping chickens and sheep and dyeing wool and knitting were all part of the cottage economy we practised. I designed them with large Russian sleeves and tight cuffs so that they wouldn't be outgrown too quickly and so that the elbows wouldn't wear out. The generous shape meant that the cardigan would fit a 2-year-old (admittedly almost down to the knees) as easily as a 6- or 7-year-old. I always knitted them in as many colours as possible, changing the colours after each set of patterning. Because they are small, the dyeing and knitting are not too daunting. Children love wearing them, and one I knitted many years ago has already been passed down from one generation to the next as if it was a family heirloom.

MATERIALS

Pair of 2¼ mm (size 13) needles
Set of 4 double-pointed 2¼ mm (size 13) needles
Pair of 3¼ mm (size 10) needles
Circular 3¼ mm (size 10) needle 40 cm (16 in) long
6 stitch holders
6 buttons

WEIGHT OF YARN AND COLOURS

400 g (14 oz) in as many colours as required

MEASUREMENTS

Length from top of shoulder to bottom edge of cardigan: 46 cm (18 in)
Actual width all round at underarm: 76 cm (30 in)
Sleeve length: 34 cm (13½ in)

TENSION

Over pattern, using 3¼ mm (size 10) needles, 31 stitches and 32 rows to 10 cm (4 in).

IMPORTANT

● The choice of colourway is entirely up to you but every panel must have a different sequence of colours. This means that each cardigan will be unique.
● Twist wools at back of work every 1–2 sts to avoid making holes, but do not pull tight.
● When working st st using just one colour twist a spare ball of the same colour yarn across the back of work to keep the thickness of the garment even.
● The sleeves are knitted on a circular needle and worked from shoulder to cuff, so remember to reverse the order of the pattern, that is, you work from row 20 to row 1.
● When knitting in the round, loop a short strand of brightly coloured wool around the first stitch each time you begin a round so that you can find the beginning easily.
● When working fronts and back the 'dots' on row 20 of pattern should be worked in the same colour as the 'dots' on rows 1–8 of following pattern, as they are part of same colour panel.

INSTRUCTIONS
FRONTS AND BACK

With 2¼ mm (size 13) needles, cast on 264 sts. Work 30 rows in k1 p1 rib, changing colours every 3 rows. Change to 3¼ mm (size 10) needles and work straight until 3 complete panels and 14 rows have been worked.

Divide for fronts and back

Row 15 With right side facing, patt 53, turn and leave rem sts on a spare needle. Work straight on these 53 sts until rows 16–20 of chart, 1 complete panel and rows 1–8 (33 rows in all) have been worked.

Neck shaping

Row 9 With right side facing, cast off 7 sts, patt to end (46 sts).

Rows 10–18 dec 1 st at neck edge every row (37 sts), then work 3 rows in background colour and slip sts onto a st holder for shoulder grafting.

Return to rem 211 sts, with right side facing slip next 24 sts onto a st holder for right underarm, patt 110 sts, then turn. Work straight in patt on these 110 sts until rows 16–20 of chart, 1 complete panel and rows 1–12 have been worked.

Row 13 patt 44 sts, k2 tog, turn and work on these 45 sts.

Rows 14–18 dec 1 st at neck edge every row.

Next 3 rows work in background colour, dec 1 st at neck edge each row (37 sts). Slip sts on to st holder for shoulder grafting.

With right side facing slip next 18 sts onto a st holder for back neck, then work rem 46 sts as follows:

Row 13 k2 tog, patt to end.

Rows 14–18 dec 1 st at neck edge every row.

Next 3 rows work in background colour, dec 1 st at neck edge of each row (37 sts). Slip sts onto st holder for shoulder grafting.

Return to rem 77 sts, and with right side facing slip next 24 sts onto a st holder for left underarm, then work straight on rem 53 sts until rows 15–20 of chart, 1 complete panel and rows 1–9 have been worked.

Row 10 With wrong side facing cast off 7 sts, patt to end (46 sts)

Rows 11–18 dec 1 st at neck edge every row, then work 3 rows in background colour, decreasing 1 st at neck edge on first of these rows (37 sts). Leave sts on needle for shoulder grafting.

Shoulder seams

Block (see page 155) garment and press carefully on wrong side using a damp cloth. With 3¼ mm (size 10) needles and wool in matching colour, graft (see page 155) right front shoulder to right back shoulder (right sides together). Rep for left shoulder. Weave in any loose ends using a darning needle (do not just cut them off).

SLEEVES

Remember sleeves are worked from shoulder to cuff.

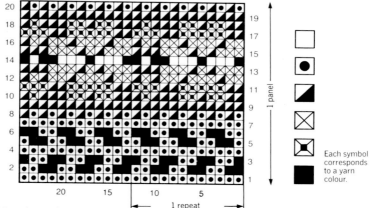

Top of garment

1 panel

1 repeat

Each symbol corresponds to a yarn colour.

Bottom of garment
Odd-numbered rows are knit, worked from right to left.
Even-numbered rows are purl, worked from left to right.

All rounds are k and chart is worked in rev order, from row 20–1.

With right side facing and 3¼ mm (size 10) circular needle and same background colour as row 9 of 6th panel of fronts and back, slip last 12 sts from st holder onto needle and k them, pick up and k 48 sts up side of armhole to shoulder seam, 48 sts down side of armhole to st holder, then slip rem 12 sts from st holder onto needle and k them (120 sts).

Next round k.

Next round k, then, beg at row 19, work 4 panels and rows 20–10 as chart.

Change to set of 4 double-pointed 2¼ mm (size 13) needles.

Dec round 1 *k1, k2 tog; rep from * to end (80 sts).

Dec round 2 *k2, k2 tog; rep from * to end (60 sts).

Work 30 rounds in k1 p1 rib, changing colour every 3 rounds and working in rev order to match Welt. Join on 2nd strand and using yarn double cast off loosely in rib. Weave in any loose ends using a darning needle and press carefully on wrong side using a damp cloth, but do not press ribbing.

BUTTONHOLE BAND

With right side facing and 2¼ mm (size 13) needles and same colour as 1st 3 rows of Welt, pick up and k 132 sts up right front edge.

Rows 1–3 work in k1 p1 rib, then make buttonholes.

Row 4 join on 2nd colour, same as 2nd colour of Welt, rib 7, cast off 5 sts, *rib 20, cast off 5 sts; rep from * to last 20 sts, rib 20.

Row 5 cont in k1 p1 rib, casting on 5 sts over the 5 buttonholes.

Row 6 work in k1 p1 rib.

Rows 7–9 join on 3rd colour, same as 3rd colour of Welt, then work in k1 p1 rib.

Row 10 p (to make foldline).

Rows 11–13 work in k1 p1 rib.

Row 14 join on 2nd colour, same as 2nd colour of Welt, then work in k1 p1 rib.

Rows 15 and 16 as rows 4 and 5.

Rows 17–19 join on 1st colour, same as 1st colour of Welt, work in k1 p1 rib, then cast off loosely in rib. Fold band to inside along foldline and stitch down neatly, neatening around buttonholes using a small buttonhole st.

BUTTONBAND

With right side facing and 2¼ mm (size 13) needles and 1st colour, pick up and k 132 sts down left front edge. Work 3 rows in k1 p1 rib, join on 2nd colour and work 3 rows in k1 p1 rib, join on 3rd colour and work 3 rows in k1 p1 rib, p next row (to make foldline), work 3 rows in k1 p1 rib, join on 2nd colour and work 3 rows in k1 p1 rib, join on 1st colour and work 3 rows in k1 p1 rib, then cast off loosely in rib. Fold band to inside along foldline and stitch down neatly. Sew on buttons.

NECKBAND

With right side facing and 2¼ mm (size 13) needles and same colour as 1st 3 rows of Welt, pick up and k 30 sts along top edge of Buttonhole band and up right front neck edge (right side facing), 12 sts down right back neck edge, 18 sts from st holder, pick up and k 12 sts up left back neck edge, 30 sts down left front neck edge and along top edge of Buttonband (102 sts).

Rows 1–3 work 3 rows in k1 p1 rib in 1st colour.

Row 4 join on 2nd colour, rib 3, cast off 5, then rib to end.

Row 5 cont in k1 p1 rib to last 3 sts, casting on 5 sts over buttonhole, rib 3.

Row 6 work in k1 p1 rib.

Rows 7–9 join on 3rd colour and work in k1 p1 rib.

Row 10 p (to make foldline).

Rows 11–13 work in k1 p1 rib.

Rows 14–15 join on 2nd colour and work as rows 4–5.

Row 16 Work in k1 p1 rib.

Rows 17–19 join on 1st colour, work in k1 p1 rib, then cast off loosely in rib.

Fold band to inside along foldline and stitch down neatly, neatening around buttonholes using a small buttonhole stitch.

AMERICAN LEAF

Early settlers in North America found the winters cold and fabrics in short supply. Housewives saved worn out clothes, which were cut up, arranged into simple patterns, lined with padding and stitched to form a quilt. This is re-cycling at its best: frugal, unpretentious, and capable of creating really stunning works of art. I have always adored patchwork quilts. An American friend gave me one that had been used by her grandmother as an under blanket and was entirely made out of men's work shirts. Our own bedspread was made by the wife of a Durham miner about a century ago. In both cases, the lack of an educated approach to design has produced an original and free piece of work. The American leaf cardigan was born out of my love of quilts, and takes its inspiration from the decorative border that usually surrounds the main design.

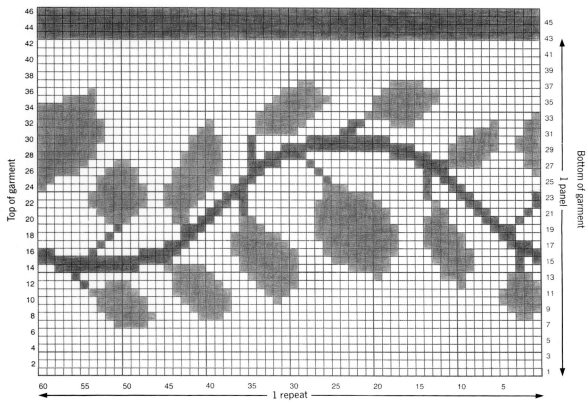

Odd-numbered rows are knit, worked from right to left.
Even-numbered rows are purl, worked from left to right.

MATERIALS

Pair of 2¼ mm (size 13) needles
Set of 4 double-pointed 2¼ mm (size 13) needles
Pair of 3¼ mm (size 10) needles
7 buttons

WEIGHT OF YARN AND COLOURS

1. Red, white and blue
Navy (A)   460 g (16 oz)
Natural (B)   230 g (8 oz)
Crimson (C)   340 g (12 oz)

2. Navy, blue and white
Navy (A)   460 g (16 oz)
Natural (B)   230 g (8 oz)
Dark Indigo blue (C)   340 g (12 oz)

MEASUREMENTS

Length from shoulder to bottom edge of cardigan:
61 cm (24 in)
Actual width all round at underarm: 147 cm (58 in)
Sleeve length: 51 cm (20 in)

TENSION

Over pattern, using 3¼ mm (size 10) needles, 30
stitches and 30 rows to 10 cm (4 in).

IMPORTANT

● Twist wools at back of work every 1–2 stitches to avoid making holes, but do not pull tight.
● When working st st using just one colour twist a spare ball of the same colour yarn across the back of work to keep the thickness of the garment even.
● This garment is knitted sideways, beginning at the left front edge, and the sleeves are also knitted sideways.
● Before beginning each new panel, check with the diagram below to ensure that you have the correct colour combination.

Key
X = background A, leaf B and stem C.
Y = background C, leaf A and stem B.
Z = background B, leaf C and stem A.

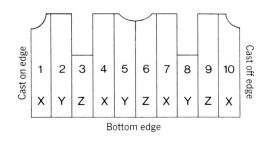

INSTRUCTIONS

FRONTS AND BACK

Panel 1
With 3¼ mm (size 10) needles and colour combination X, cast on 126 sts in A and work from chart, beg at st 1, row 1.
Rows 1–12 as chart.
Neck shaping
Row 13 With right side facing inc 1 st at end (neck edge) of row.
Rows 14–16 as chart.
Rows 17–29 inc 1 st at end (neck edge) of this and next 6 alternate rows (134 sts).
Rows 30–31 as chart.
Row 32 With wrong side facing cast on 15 sts (neck edge), patt to end (149 sts).
Rows 33–42 as chart, then work 4 rows rev st st in A as follows:
Row 1 k.
Row 2 k.
Row 3 p.
Row 4 k.

Panel 2
Using colour combination Y, work from chart.
Rows 1–41 as chart.

Row 42 With wrong side facing cast off 52 sts (neck edge), patt to end (97 sts). Then join on A and work 4 rows rev st st as before.

Panel 3 (underarm panel)
Using colour combination Z, work from chart.
Rows 1–42 as chart, then join on A and work 4 rows rev st st as before.

Panel 4
Using colour combination X, work from chart.
Row 1 With right side facing, patt to end of row (neck edge) then cast on 52 sts (149 sts).
Rows 2–42 as chart, then work 4 rows rev st st in A as before.

Panel 5
Using colour combination Y, work from chart.
Rows 1–10 as chart.
Rows 11–15 dec 1 st at end (neck edge) of this and next 2 alternate rows (146 sts).
Rows 16–42 as chart, then join on A and work 4 rows rev st st as before.

Panel 6
Using colour combination Z, work from chart.
Rows 1–26 as chart.
Rows 27–31 inc 1 st at end (neck edge) of this and next 2 alternate rows (149 sts).
Rows 32–42 as chart, then join on A and work 4 rows rev st st as before.

Panel 7
Using colour combination X, work from chart.
Rows 1–41 as chart.
Row 42 With wrong side facing cast off 52 sts (neck edge), patt to end (97 sts), then work 4 rows rev st st in A as before.

Panel 8 (underarm panel)
Using colour combination Y, work from chart.
Rows 1–42 as chart, then join on A and work 4 rows rev st st as before.

Panel 9
Using colour combination Z, work from chart.
Row 1 With right side facing patt to end of row (neck edge) and cast on 52 sts (149 sts).
Rows 2–42 as chart, then join on A and work 4 rows rev st st as before.

Panel 10
Using colour combination X, work from chart.
Rows 1–11 as chart.
Neck shaping
Row 12 With wrong side facing cast off 15 sts, patt to end (134 sts).

Rows 13–14 as chart.
Rows 15–27 dec 1 st at end (neck edge) of this and next 6 alternate rows (127 sts).
Rows 28–30 as chart.
Row 31 dec 1 st at end (neck edge) of row (126 sts).
Rows 32–42 as chart, then cast off loosely.
Weave in any loose ends using a darning needle (do not just cut them off). Block (see page 155) garment and press carefully on wrong side using a damp cloth.

Shoulder seams
With right side facing and 2¼ mm (size 13) needles and A, pick up and k 52 sts along right front shoulder. K 1 row, p 1 row, k 1 row. Leave sts on a spare needle for grafting. With right side facing and 2¼ mm (size 13) needles and A, pick up and k 52 sts along right back shoulder and leave sts on needle for grafting. Graft (see page 155) right front shoulder to right back shoulder (right sides together). Rep for left shoulder.

SLEEVES
Left sleeve
With 3¼ mm (size 10) needles and B, cast on 123 sts. Work 6 complete panels with 4 rows rev st st in A between each panel with colour combinations in following order:
Panel 1 (underarm panel) Z.
Panel 2 X.
Panel 3 Y.
Panel 4 Z.
Panel 5 X.
Panel 6 Y.
Then work 4 rows rev st st in A and keep sts on needle. Weave in any loose ends using a darning needle (do not just cut them off). Press carefully on wrong side using a damp cloth, then graft (see page 155) cast on edge to sts on needle.

Right sleeve
Work as Left sleeve, but in following colour combinations:
Panel 1 (underarm panel) Y.
Panel 2 Z.
Panel 3 X.
Panel 4 Y.
Panel 5 Z.
Panel 6 X.

Cuffs
With right side facing and set of 4 double-pointed 2¼ mm (size 13) needles and A, pick up and k 160 sts around lower edge of sleeve (making sure leaves are pointing down to cuff). Loop short strand brightly coloured wool round 1st st of each round so that you can find beg of round easily.
Round 1 *k2 tog; rep from * to end (80 sts).
Round 2 *k2, k2 tog; rep from * to end (60 sts).

Work 32 rounds in k1 p1 rib, then join on 2nd strand A and using yarn double cast off loosely in rib.

WELT
With right side facing and 2¼ mm (size 13) needles and A, pick up and k 230 sts along lower edge of fronts and back. Work 32 rows in k1 p1 rib, then join on 2nd strand A and using yarn double cast off loosely in rib.

NECKBAND
With right side facing and 2¼ mm (size 13) needles and A, pick up and k 100 sts around neck. Work 9 rows in k1 p1 rib, k 2 rows (to make foldline), then work 9 rows more in k1 p1 rib. Cast off loosely in rib.

BUTTONHOLE BAND
With right side facing and 2¼ mm (size 13) needles and A, pick up and k 180 sts up right front edge.
Rows 1–4 work in k1 p1 rib, then make buttonholes.
Row 5 rib 6, *cast off 6 sts, rib 21 including st already on needle; rep from * to last 12 sts, cast off 6 sts, rib 6.
Row 6 work in k1 p1 rib, casting on 6 sts over the 7 buttonholes.
Rows 7–9 work in k1 p1 rib.
Rows 10 and 11 k (to make foldline).
Rows 12–14 work in k1 p1 rib.
Rows 15 and 16 as rows 5 and 6.
Rows 17–20 work in k1 p1 rib, then cast off loosely in rib. Fold band to inside along foldline and stitch down neatly, neatening around buttonholes using a small buttonhole st.

BUTTONBAND
With right side facing and 2¼ mm (size 13) needles and A, pick up and k 180 sts down left front edge. Work 9 rows in k1 p1 rib, k 2 rows (to make foldline), then work 9 more rows in k1 p1 rib and cast off loosely in rib. Fold band to inside along foldline and stitch down neatly. Sew on buttons.

SLEEVE INSERTION
Make 3 pleats in top of left sleeve by folding rev st st at top edge of panel 5 to centre of panel 5, rev st st at top edge of panel 4 to centre of panel 4 and rev st st at top edge of panel 3 to centre of panel 3. On right sleeve fold rev st st at top edge of panel 2 to centre of panel 3, panel 3 to panel 4 and panel 4 to panel 5. Stitch the pleats down neatly (check that pleats face front of garment and that underarm panel is in the same colour combination as underarm panel on body). With right side facing and set of 4 double-pointed 2¼ mm (size 13) needles and A, pick up and k 110 sts around top edge of sleeve and p 3 rounds. Leave sts on needle. Place sleeve in armhole (right sides together), matching underarm panels and middle pleat with shoulder seam, and graft (see page 155) tog. Weave in any rem loose ends using a darning needle (do not just cut them off).

PLAITED BAND

MATERIALS
Pair of 4½ mm (size 7) needles
3 strips approximately 100 by 6 cm (3 ft 4 in by 2¼ in)
of 115 g (4 oz) polyester wadding

WEIGHT OF YARN AND COLOURS
Natural (A)   57 g (2 oz)
Navy (B)   57 g (2 oz)
Crimson (C)   57 g (2 oz)

TENSION
Over stocking stitch, using 4½ mm (size 7 needles), 25
stitches and 24 rows to 10 cm (4 in).

INSTRUCTIONS

BAND 1
With 4½ mm (size 7) needles and A, cast on 112 sts.
Work 26 rows in st st, then cast off loosely.

BAND 2
As Band 1, but work in B.

BAND 3
As Band 1, but work in C.
Weave in any loose ends on all Bands using a darning
needle (do not just cut them off), then press on wrong
side using a damp cloth.

FINISHING
Lay Band 1 (wrong side up) on a flat surface and lay one
of the strips of wadding down the centre.
Bring each side of band up over wadding to meet along
centre and oversew edges neatly in A.
Rep these 2 stages for Bands 2 and 3, oversewing in B
and C respectively.
Then plait the Bands tog – firmly but not too tightly –
and bring ends of plait tog to form a circle.
Stitch ends of wadding tog, then oversew ends of Band
1 tog neatly and rep for Bands 2 and 3. Adjust plait so
that seams are inside or under another Band.

PAISLEY

A long-time favourite and a true classic. The paisley motif combines a floral design from woven Indian shawls, a Persian vase of flowers and, less exotically, the stylized pine pattern used on the shawls produced in the Scottish town of Paisley in the 19th century. Despite the apparent simplicity, it was difficult to translate onto graph paper in a way that would be easy to knit, and I spent hours drawing paisley designs before finding one that worked well on a jacket. I have used three colours in a row, and it is important to keep the tension even and weave the wool on every stitch. The navy background can be dyed in one go by multiplying the recipe by five.

MATERIALS

Pair of 2¼ mm (size 13) needles
Set of 4 double-pointed 2¼ mm (size 13) needles
Pair of 3¼ mm (size 10) needles
Circular 3¼ mm (size 10) needle 40 cm (16 in) long
9 stitch holders
7 buttons

WEIGHT OF YARN AND COLOURS

Navy (A)   560 g (20 oz)
Crimson (B1)   230 g (8 oz)
Red (B2)   230 g (8 oz)
Grass green (C)   170 g (6 oz)

MEASUREMENTS

Length from top of shoulder to bottom edge of jacket:
86.5 cm (34 in)
Actual width all round at underarm: 127 cm (50 in)
Sleeve length: 57 cm (22½ in)

TENSION

Over pattern, using 3¼ mm (size 10) needles, 30 stitches and 28 rows to 10 cm (4 in).

Bottom of garment

Odd-numbered rows are knit, worked from right to left.
Even-numbered rows are purl, worked from left to right.

IMPORTANT

● The pattern is staggered, therefore begin panel 1 at stitch 1, row 1; panel 2 at stitch 31, row 1; panel 3 at stitch 61, row 1; panel 4 at stitch 11, row 1; panel 5 at stitch 41, row 1; panel 6 at stitch 71, row 1; panel 7 at stitch 21, row 1; panel 8 at stitch 51, row 1; panel 9 as panel 1 and so on (chart shows the first 3 panels).

● Change shade of red every 2–3 rows to give a random effect.

● Twist wools at back of work every 1–2 stitches to avoid making holes, but do not pull tight.

● When working st st using just one colour twist a spare ball of the same colour yarn across the back of work to keep the thickness of the garment even.

● When using the circular needle for the sleeves,

remember that all rounds of chart are knit and must be worked in reverse order as you are knitting from shoulder to cuff, that is, you work from row 22 to 1.

● When using the circular needle, loop a short strand of brightly coloured wool around the first stitch each time you begin a round so that you can find the beginning easily.

INSTRUCTIONS
FRONTS AND BACK

With 2¼ mm (size 13) needles and 2 strands A (to give a firmer edge), cast on 310 sts. Cont with 1 strand A and work in k1 p1 rib as follows:

Rows 1–4 work in A.
Rows 5–8 work in B.

Rows 9 and 10 work in C.
Rows 11–14 work in B.
Rows 15–16 work in A.
Rows 17–20 work in C.
Rows 21–22 work in B.
Rows 23–26 work in C.
Rows 27–28 work in A.
Rows 29–32 work in B.
Rows 33–34 work in C.
Rows 35–38 work in B.
Rows 39–41 work in A.
Next row (wrong side facing) *rib 4, inc into next st; rep from* to end (372 sts).
Next row change to 3¼ mm (size 10) needles, k1, then work from chart, beg at st 1, row 1, to last st, k1.

(Omit small motifs on 1st 2 rows.)

Next row p 1, patt to last st, p1.

Cont as chart, keeping 1st and last sts plain as these are the front edges, and work 2 complete panels (44 rows).

Pocket linings

Lay work on one side. With 3¼ mm (size 10) needles and A, cast on 42 sts. For Pocket lining 1, beg at st 28, row 1 of chart, for Pocket lining 2, beg at st 62, row 1 and work 2 complete panels. Leave sts on spare needles. Return to main body of work. Patt 28 sts, slip next 42 sts onto a st holder for pocket top, then join in Pocket lining 1, k from its needle, keeping patt correct, and patt to last 70 sts. Slip next 42 sts onto a st holder for pocket top, then join in Pocket lining 2, k from its needle, keeping patt correct, and patt to end. Work straight until 6 complete panels have been worked.

Divide for fronts and back

With right side facing patt 70 sts, turn. Cont in patt on these 70 sts until 8 complete panels have been worked from beg.

Next row cast off 16 sts for neck, patt to end (54 sts).

Next row row 2 of chart.

Row 3 cast off 2 sts, patt to end.

Row 4 as chart.

Row 5 cast off 2 sts, patt to end.

Row 6 as chart.

Rows 7–17 dec 1 st at beg (neck edge) of this and next 5 alternate rows (44 sts).

Work straight in patt until 9 panels have been worked from beg, then slip sts onto a st holder for right shoulder grafting. Return to rem sts, slip next 46 sts onto a st holder for right underarm, then patt next 140 sts for back and turn. Work straight on these 140 sts until 8 complete panels and 14 rows have been worked from beg.

Next row With right side facing patt 49, k2 tog, k1, turn.

Next row p1, p2 tog, patt to end.

Next row patt to last 3 sts, k2 tog, k1.

Rep last 2 rows until 44 sts rem (9 complete panels have now been worked), then slip sts onto a st holder for right back shoulder grafting. Slip next 36 sts onto a st holder for back neck and work rem 52 sts as follows: k1, k2 tog, patt to end.

Next row patt to last 3 sts, p2 tog, p1.

Next row k1, k2 tog, patt to end.

Rep last 2 rows until 44 sts rem (9 complete panels have now been worked), then slip sts onto a st holder for left back shoulder grafting. Slip next 46 sts onto a st holder for left underarm and then patt rem 70 sts.

Work straight on these sts until 8 complete panels and 1 row of chart have been worked from beg.

Row 2 cast off 16 sts, patt to end (54 sts).

Row 3 as chart.

Row 4 cast off 2 sts, patt to end.

Row 5 as chart.

Row 6 cast off 2 sts, patt to end.

Row 7 as chart.

Rows 8–18 dec 1 st at beg (neck edge) of this and next 5 alternate rows (44 sts).

Work straight in patt until 9 complete panels have been worked, then slip sts onto a st holder for left front shoulder grafting.

Pocket tops

With right side facing and 2¼ mm (size 13) needles and A, slip sts for pocket from st holder onto needle and work in k1 p1 rib as follows:

Rows 1 and 2 work in A.

Rows 3–6 work in B.

Rows 7 and 8 work in C.

Rows 9–10 work in B.

Rows 11 and 12 work in A then cast off loosely in rib using 2 strands A. Block (see page 155) garment and press carefully on wrong side using a damp cloth, but do not press ribbing. Stitch down pocket tops neatly and sew Pocket linings into place using a small slip st.

Shoulder seams

Graft (see page 155) right front shoulder to right back shoulder (right sides together). Rep for other shoulder. Press carefully on wrong side using a damp cloth, but do not press ribbing.

SLEEVES

Remember to k all rounds and work panels in rev order – from row 22–1.

With right side facing and a 3¼ mm (size 10) circular needle and A, slip last 23 sts for underarm from st holder onto needle and k them. Then pick up and k 114 sts around armhole and k rem 23 sts from st holder (160 sts). Working from chart in rev order, cont until 6 panels have been worked. Cont with A.

Next round *k2, k2 tog; rep from * to end (120 sts).

Next round change to set of 4 double-pointed 2¼ mm (size 13) needles and *k2 tog; rep from * to end (60

sts). Then work 45 rounds in k1 p1 rib following colour sequence of rib given at beg of instructions for fronts and back, but in rev order and working 4 rows instead of 2 in the A stripes. Cast off in rib using 2 strands A. Weave in any loose ends using a darning needle (do not just cut them off) and press carefully on wrong side using a damp cloth, but do not press ribbing.

NECKBAND

With right side facing and 2¼ mm (size 13) needles and A, pick up and k 110 sts around neck, including sts on holder at back neck. Working in k1 p1 rib work 2 rows A, 4 rows B, 2 rows C, 4 rows B and 2 rows A then cast off loosely in rib using 2 strands A.

BUTTONHOLE BAND

With right side facing and 2¼ mm (size 13) needles and A, pick up and k 210 sts up right front edge of jacket.

Rows 1 and 2 work in k1 p1 rib in A.

Rows 3–6 work in k1 p1 rib in B, then make buttonholes.

Row 7 working in C, rib 3, cast off 6 sts, *rib 27, including st left on needle, cast off 6; rep from * to last 3 sts, rib 3.

Row 8 cont in C in k1 p1 rib, casting on 6 sts over the 7 buttonholes.

Rows 9–12 work in k1 p1 rib in B.

Rows 13 and 14 work in k1 p1 rib in A, then cast off loosely in rib using 2 strands A.

Using strand of C, neaten around buttonholes using a small buttonhole st.

BUTTONBAND

With right side facing and 2¼ mm (size 13) needles and A, pick up and k 210 sts down left front edge of jacket. Work in k1 p1 rib as given for rows 1–14 of neckband above. Cast off loosely in rib using 2 strands A. Sew on buttons.

PAISLEY HAT

MATERIALS

Pair of 5 mm (size 6) needles
4 mm (size 8) crochet hook
Approximately 130 by 10 cm (3 ft 12¾ in by 4 in) strip
of 115 g (4oz) polyester wadding

WEIGHT OF YARN AND COLOURS

PLIED YARN   (or 2 strands of ordinary yarn knitted
together)
Navy (A)   115 g (4 oz)
Grass green (B)   115 g (4 oz)
Crimson (C)   115 g (4 oz)

TENSION

Over pattern, using 5 mm (size 6) needles, 16 stitches
and 24 rows to 10 cm (4 in).

INSTRUCTIONS
BRIM

With 5 mm (size 6) needles and A, cast on 60 sts. Work
in st st.
Row 1 k.
Row 2 p.
Row 3 join on B, inc 1 st at beg of row and dec 1 st at
end of row.
Row 4 p.
Rows 5–9 Rep rows 3 and 4 twice and row 3 once.
Row 10 join on A and p.
Rows 11–17 join on C and shape as rows 3 and 4.
Rows 2–17 form stripe pattern. Rep 4 more times and
then cast off loosely. Weave in any loose ends using a
darning needle (do not just cut them off) and press
carefully on wrong side using a damp cloth. Bring cast
on edge and cast off edge tog (right sides tog) and sew
neat seam using small back stitches.

CROWN

With right side facing and 5 mm (size 6) needles and A,
cast on 104 sts and work 22 rows in st st, then shape as
follows:
Row 1 k5, k3 tog, *k10, k3 tog; rep from * to last 5 sts,
k5 (88 sts).
Rows 2–6 work in st st.
Row 7 k4, k3 tog, *k8, k3 tog; rep from * to last 4 sts,
k4 (72 sts).
Rows 8–12 work in st st.
Row 13 k3, k3 tog, *k6, k3 tog; rep from * to last 3 sts,
k3 (56 sts).
Rows 14–18 work in st st.
Row 19 k2, k3 tog, *k4, k3 tog; rep from * to last 2 sts,
k2 (40 sts).
Rows 20–25 work in st st.
Row 26 k1, k3 tog, *k2, k3 tog; rep from * to last st,
k1 (26 sts).
Row 27 *k2 tog; rep from * to end (13 sts). Keep sts

on needle. Cut off wool, leaving a length of about 15 cm
(5¾ in), then, using a darning needle, thread this
through sts on needle, pull tightly and fasten off
securely. Bring side edges of crown tog (right sides tog)
and sew neat seam using small back stitches.

FLAPS
Right flap lining

With 5 mm (size 6) needles and B, cast on 30 sts and
work 100 rows in st st.
Next row *k3 tog; rep to end of row (10 sts). Cut off
wool, leaving a length of about 15 cm (5¾ in), then,
using a darning needle, thread this through sts on
needle, pull tightly and fasten off securely. Rep for Left
flap lining, but work in C.

Right outer flap

With 5 mm (size 6) needles and A, cast on 30 sts and
work 100 rows as chart.
Next row *k3 tog; rep to end of row (10 sts). Fasten off
as Flap linings above. Rep for Left outer flap.

FINISHING
Flaps

Place Right outer flap on Right flap lining (right sides tog)
and sew neat seam using small back stitches all round
flap, except for cast on edges, then turn right side out
and stitch cast on edges of each flap tog neatly. Rep for
Left outer flap and Left flap lining.

Tassels

(See page 157 for Crochet instructions.) With 4 mm
(size 8) crochet hook and A, make 2 braids 40 ch in
length. Cut 60 lengths of B and 60 lengths of C, each
approximately 30 cm (11¾ in).
Fold the 60 lengths of B over the centre of one of the
crocheted braids, then wind a strand of B several times
tightly around lengths of B, forming tassel, and tie a tight
knot. With a strand of A, stitch the crocheted braid
immediately above top of tassel. Then, pass the 2 ends
of the crocheted braid through the small hole at the
gathered end of the flap and stitch firmly in place on
wrong side. Rep for 2nd tassel in C.

Joining brim and crown

Place edge of brim approximately 2 cm (3¼ in) above
cast on edge of crown (right sides tog) and stitch a neat
seam using small back stitches. Place Right flap 5 cm
(2 in) away from seam in crown (lining and wrong side
of crown tog, cast on edges aligned) and sew neat seam
using small back sts. Rep for Left flap.
Fold wadding in half lengthways and lay it on wrong side
of brim below seam. Bring unsewn edge of brim down
over wadding and slip stitch it carefully to cast on edge
of crown and right side of Flaps, turning edge of brim
under as you do so for a neat finish.

Cast off edge

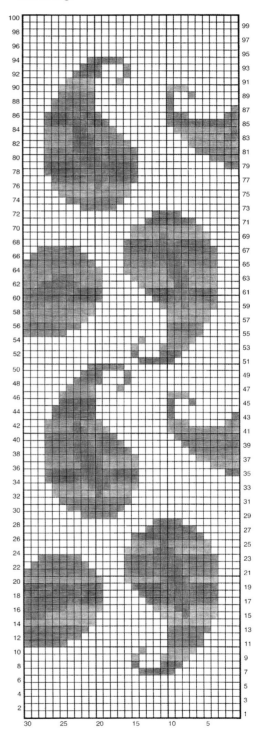

Cast on edge
Odd-numbered rows are knit, worked from right to left.
Even-numbered rows are purl, worked from left to right.

FOUR-LEAF CLOVER

'With a four leav'd clover, double topp'd ash, and green tipp'd seave
You may go before the queen's daughter without ever asking leave.'

Ash and green rushes are no longer thought of as lucky, but the four-leaf clover remains as strong a symbol of good fortune as ever. As a family, we always hunt for one when in a meadow or on a picnic, and the thrill of discovery is as memorable now as it was when I was a child.

   The clovers climb the cardigan, and the natural greens blend together in infinite variations. The dark grey ruffles dividing the panels create a rippled effect against the grey background. It is possible to dye all the 460 g (16 oz) of grey needed in one go by using a larger saucepan and multiplying the quantities of dye and mordant given in the recipe by four.

MATERIALS
Pair of 2¼ mm (size 13) needles
Set of 4 double-pointed 2¼ mm (size 13) needles
Pair of 3¼ mm (size 10) needles
Set of 4 double-pointed 3¼ mm (size 10) needles
6 buttons

WEIGHT OF YARN AND COLOURS
Grey (A)   460 g (16 oz)
Dark grey (B)   170 g (6 oz)
Grass green (C1)   115 g (4 oz)
Olive green (C2)   115 g (4 oz)
Blue green (C3)   115 g (4 oz)

MEASUREMENTS
Length from top of shoulder to bottom edge of jacket:
68.5 cm (27 in)
Actual width all round at underarm: 127 cm (50 in)
Sleeve length: 57 cm (22½ in)

TENSION
Over pattern, using 3¼ mm (size 10) needles, 28 sts and 28 rows to 10 cm (4 in).

Top of garment

42 40 38 36 34 32 30 28 26 24 22 20 18 16 14 12 10 8 6 4 2

41 39 37 35 33 31 29 27 25 23 21 19 17 15 13 11 9 7 5 3 1

Bottom of garment 1 panel

90 85 80 75 70 65 60 55 50 45 40 35 30 25 20 15 10 5

1 repeat

Odd-numbered rows are knit, worked from right to left.

Even-numbered rows are purl, worked from left to right.

IMPORTANT

- Twist wools at back of work every 1–2 stitches to avoid making holes, but do not pull tight.
- When working st st using just one colour twist a spare ball of the same colour yarn across the back of work to keep the thickness of the garment even.
- Change colours of four-leaf clover motif every 2–3 rows to give a random effect.
- This garment is knitted sideways, beginning at the left front edge, and the sleeves are also knitted sideways.
- The frills are added after the fronts and back and the sleeves have been worked.

INSTRUCTIONS
FRONTS AND BACK

Panel 1
With 3¼ mm (size 10) needles and A, cast on 146 sts.
Row 1 k (right side facing).
Row 2 p.
Row 3 work from chart, beg at st 1, row 21.
Rows 22–26 as chart.
Cont working from chart, inc on each alternate row as follows:
Rows 27 and 29 inc 1 st at end (neck edge) of row.
Rows 31 and 33 cast on 2 sts at end (neck edge) of row.

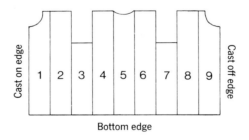

Cast on edge

1 2 3 4 5 6 7 8 9

Cast off edge

Bottom edge

Rows 35 and 37 cast on 3 sts at end (neck edge) of row.
Rows 39 and 41 cast on 5 sts at end (neck edge) of row (168 sts).
Row 42 as chart, then join on B, k 2 rows and cut off B.

Panel 2
Cont in A and work from chart, beg at st 1, row 1.
Rows 1–41 as chart.
Row 42 With wrong side facing cast off 52 sts (neck edge), patt to end (116 sts), then join on B, k 2 rows and cut off B.

Panel 3 (underarm panel)
Cont in A and work rows 1–42 as chart, beg at st 1, row 1, then join on B, k 2 rows and cut off B.

Panel 4
Cont in A and work from chart, beg at st 1, row 1.
Row 1 Patt to end of row (neck edge) then cast on 52 sts (168 sts).
Rows 2–42 as chart, then join on B, k 2 rows and cut off B.

Panel 5
Cont in A and work from chart, beg at st 1, row 1, dec and inc as follows:
Row 1 With right side facing dec 1 st at end (neck edge) of row.
Row 4 dec 1 st at beg (neck edge) of row.
Row 8 dec 1 st at beg (neck edge) of row.
Row 12 dec 1 st at beg (neck edge) of row.
Rows 13–29 work straight as chart.
Row 30 With wrong side facing inc 1 st at beg (neck edge) of row.
Row 34 inc 1 st at beg (neck edge) of row.
Row 38 inc 1 st at beg (neck edge) of row.
Row 42 inc 1 st at beg (neck edge) of row (168 sts), then join on B, k 2 rows and cut off B.

Panel 6
Cont in A and work from chart, beg at st 1, row 1.
Rows 1–41 as chart.
Row 42 cast off 52 sts (neck edge), patt to end (116 sts), then join on B, k 2 rows and cut off B.

Panel 7 (underarm panel)

Cont in A and work from chart, beg at st 1, row 1.
Rows 1–42 as chart, then join on B, k 2 rows and cut off B.

Panel 8

Cont in A and work from chart, beg at st 1, row 1.
Row 1 Patt to end of row (neck edge) then cast on 52 sts (168 sts).
Rows 2–42 as chart, then join on B, k 2 rows and cut off B.

Panel 9

Cont in A and work from chart, beg at st 1, row 1, dec on each alternate row as follows:
Rows 2 and 4 cast off 5 sts (neck edge), patt to end.
Rows 6 and 8 cast off 3 sts (neck edge), patt to end.
Rows 10 and 12 cast off 2 sts (neck edge), patt to end.
Rows 14 and 16 cast off 1 st (neck edge), patt to end (146 sts).
Rows 17–22 as chart. With A, k 1 row, p 1 row then cast off loosely. Weave in any loose ends using a darning needle (do not just cut them off) then block (see page 000) garment and press carefully on wrong side using a damp cloth.

Frills

With right side facing and 2¼ mm (size 13) needles and B, pick up and k 168 sts along 2 k rows in B between Panels 1 and 2. Work 2 rows in k1 p1 rib, then change to 3¼ mm (size 10) needles and work 1 row inc into every st (336 sts).
Next row work in k1 p1 rib.
Next row k, then cast off loosely purlwise.
Rep for each 2 k rows in B between panels, but pick up and k 116 sts instead of 168 either side of Panels 3 and 7.

Shoulder seams

With right side facing and 2¼ mm (size 13) needles and B, pick up and k 40 sts along right front shoulder, k 1 row and leave sts on a spare needle for grafting.
With right side facing and 2¼ mm (size 13) needles and B, pick up and k 40 sts along right back shoulder and leave sts on needle for grafting. Graft (see page 155) right front shoulder to right back shoulder (right sides together).
Frill Pick up and k 40 sts (not 168) along shoulder seam and work as before.
Rep for 2nd shoulder.
Using darning needle and short strand B, fasten down ends of Shoulder frills and Frills of fronts and back by passing needle up through work, through end cast off st of frill and back through work, pulling tightly so frill curves in to work.

SLEEVES

With 3¼ mm (size 10) needles and A, cast on 133 sts and work 4 complete panels as chart with 2 k rows in B

between each panel and end with 2 k rows in B. Keep sts on needle. Press carefully on wrong side using a damp cloth and graft (see page 155) sts on needle to cast on edge of sleeve (right sides together).

Frills

Work as before, but pick up and k 133 sts instead of 168.

Cuffs

With right side facing and set of 4 double-pointed 2¼ mm (size 13) needles and B, pick up and k 122 sts around lower edge of sleeve, ensuring patt is right way up. When picking up sts, pick up a st through end cast off st of each frill and pull tightly so it curves in to cuff to neaten.
Round 1 *k2 tog; rep from * to end (61 sts).
Round 2 *k4, k2 tog; rep from * to last 7 sts, k4, k3 tog (50 sts), then work 24 more rounds in k1 p1 rib. Loop short strand brightly coloured wool around 1st st of round as a marker and then work 2 rounds in k1 p1 rib.
Frill 1 Change to set of 4 double-pointed 3¼ mm (size 10) needles and work 1 round, inc into every st (100 sts).
Next round work in k1 p1 rib.
Next round p, then cast off loosely knitwise.
Frill 2 With set of 4 double-pointed 2¼ mm (size 13) needles and B, pick up and k 50 sts along round indicated by marker on inside of cuff. Work 3 rounds in k1 p1 rib, then loop short strand brightly coloured wool round 1st st of round. Work 2 more rounds in k1 p1 rib. Then, change to set of 4 double-pointed 3¼ mm (size 10) needles and work 1 round, inc into every st (100 sts).
Next round work in k1 p1 rib.
Next round p, then cast off loosely knitwise.
Frill 3 With set of 4 double-pointed 2¼ mm (size 13) needles and B, pick up and k 50 sts along round indicated by 2nd marker on inside of cuff. Work 5 rounds in k1 p1 rib, then change to set of 4 double-pointed 3¼ mm (size 10) needles and work 1 round, inc into every st (100 sts).
Next round work in k1 p1 rib.
Next round p, then cast off loosely knitwise.

WELT

With right side facing and 2¼ mm (size 13) needles and B, pick up and k 230 sts along lower edge of fronts and back, picking up a st through end cast off st of each frill, pulling it tightly so it curves in to welt as you do so to neaten. Work 25 rows in k1 p1 rib. Join on 2nd strand B and using yarn double cast off loosely in rib.

NECKBAND

With right side facing and 2¼ mm (size 13) needles and B, pick up and k 110 sts around neck. Work 5 rows in k1 p1 rib.
Frill 1 Change to 3¼ mm (size 10) needles and work 1

row, inc into every st, and then pick up and k 4 sts down side of ribbing (224 sts).
Next row work in k1 p1 rib and then pick up and k 4 sts down side of ribbing (228 sts). K 2 rows, then cast off loosely purlwise.
Frill 2 Turn Frill 1 down on to right side of work and with 2¼ mm (size 13) needles and B, pick up and k 110 sts on inside of neck in exactly the same place as Frill 1, then work 7 rows in k1 p1 rib. Change to 3¼ mm (size 10) needles and work 1 row, inc into every st and then pick up and k 6 sts down side of ribbing (226 sts).
Next row work in k1 p1 rib and then pick up and k 6 sts down side of ribbing (232 sts). K 2 rows, then cast off loosely purlwise.
Frill 3 Turn Frills 1 and 2 down on to right side of work and with 2¼ mm (size 13) needles and B, pick up and k 110 sts on inside of neck in exactly the same place as Frills 1 and 2, then work 11 rows in k1 p1 rib. Change to 3¼ mm (size 10) needles and work 1 row, inc into every st and then pick up and k 10 sts down side of ribbing (230 sts).
Next row work in k1 p1 rib and then pick up and k 10 sts down side of ribbing (240 sts). K 2 rows, then cast off loosely purlwise.

BUTTONHOLE BAND

With right side facing and 2¼ mm (size 13) needles and B, pick up and k 172 sts up right front edge.
Rows 1–3 work in k1 p1 rib, then make buttonholes.
Row 4 rib 3, cast off 6 sts, *rib 26 including st already on needle, cast off 6 sts; rep from * to last 3 sts, rib 3.
Row 5 cont in k1 p1 rib, casting on 6 sts over the 6 buttonholes.
Rows 6–9 work in k1 p1 rib.
Row 10 p (to make foldline).
Rows 11–14 work in k1 p1 rib.
Rows 15 and 16 as rows 4 and 5.
Rows 17–19 work in k1 p1 rib, then cast off loosely in rib. Fold band to inside along foldline and stitch down neatly, neatening around buttonholes using a small buttonhole st.

BUTTONBAND

With right side facing and 2¼ mm (size 13) needles and B, pick up and k 172 sts down left front edge. Work 9 rows in k1 p1 rib, p next row (to make foldline), work 9 more rows in k1 p1 rib, then cast off loosely in rib. Fold band to inside along foldline and stitch down neatly. Sew on buttons.

ARMHOLE FRILLS

With right side facing and set of 4 double-pointed 2¼ mm (size 13) needles and B, pick up and k 122 sts along 2nd row in of 3 of the panels at top of sleeve (4th panel is the underarm panel). Work 2 rows in k1 p1 rib, then change to set of 4 double-pointed 3¼ mm (size 10) needles and inc into every st (244 sts).
Next row work in k1 p1 rib.
Next row k, then cast off loosely purlwise.

SLEEVE INSERTION

Place sleeve in armhole with right sides tog, matching
underarm panel and making sure Frill is turned down on
right side of sleeve. Sew neat seam using small back sts.
Weave in any rem loose ends using a darning needle
and press carefully on wrong side using a damp cloth.
Do not press ribbing or frills.

FRITILLARY

We live on the edge of water meadows, and the ground is always damp, making it a perfect habitat for fritillaries. They have a delicacy I adore, and a host of popular names, of which Chequered Lily is my own favourite. For this design I have paired the flowers, making the edging checked as well. It is a large piece of knitting, which can be ruined by uneven tension and by not twisting the wool properly across the back. The ribs, pocket edges, shoulder ruffles and button bands are very strong, as they are all both Fair Isle and knitted double.

MATERIALS
Pair of 2¼ mm (size 13) needles
Set of 4 double-pointed 2¼ mm (size 13) needles
2 pairs of 3¼ mm (size 10) needles
Circular 3¼ mm (size 10) needle 40 cm (16 in) long
8 stitch holders
7 buttons

WEIGHT OF YARN AND COLOURS
Dark grey (A)   500 g (18 oz)
Natural (B)   230 g (8 oz)
Crimson (C)   170 g (6 oz)
Grass green (D)   170 g (6 oz)

MEASUREMENTS
Length from top of shoulder to bottom edge of jacket:
89 cm (35 in)
Actual width all round at underarm: 127 cm (50 in)
Sleeve length: 57 cm (22½ in)

TENSION
Over pattern, using 3¼ mm (size 10) needles, 30
stitches and 30 rows to 10 cm (4 in).

IMPORTANT
● Twist wools at back of work every 1–2 stitches to
avoid making holes, but do not pull tight.
● When working st st using just one colour twist a
spare ball of the same colour yarn across the back of
work to keep the thickness of the garment even.
● When using the circular needle, loop a short strand
of brightly coloured wool around the first stitch so that
you can find the beginning of each round easily.
● The sleeves are knitted from shoulder to wrist so the
panels must be worked in reverse order, that is, you
work from round 28 to 1.

CHART A

Top of garment

Bottom of garment

Odd-numbered rows are knit, worked from right to left.
Even-numbered rows are purl, worked from left to right.

CHART B

INSTRUCTIONS
FRONTS AND BACK
With 2¼ mm (size 13) needles and A, cast on 320 sts and work 32 rows from chart B.

Next row k in A.

Next row k in A (to make foldline), then beginning at st 1, row 5, work 32 more rows from chart B. Change to 3¼ mm (size 10) needles.

Inc row work row 1 of chart A in A and at the same time, k6, *k6, inc into next st; rep from * to last 6 sts, k6 (364 sts). Cont working from chart A until 2 panels have been worked.

Pockets
Lay work on one side and work Pocket linings. With 3¼ mm (size 10) needles and A, cast on 42 sts and work from chart A, beginning at st 29, row 1, until 2 complete panels have been worked. Keep sts on one of 2nd pair of 3¼ mm needles. Rep for 2nd Pocket lining, beginning at st 7, row 1. Return to main body of work and cont as follows. Patt 28 sts, slip next 42 sts onto a st holder, then join on 1st Pocket lining, knitting from its needle, keeping to patt, and patt to last 70 sts. Slip next 42 sts onto a st holder, then join on 2nd Pocket lining, knitting from its needle, keeping to patt, and patt to end. Cont working from chart A until 5 panels and 14 rows have been worked from the beginning.

Divide for fronts and back
With right side facing patt 70 sts, turn. Cont on these sts until 7 panels and 6 rows have been worked from the beginning.

Neck shaping
Row 7 With right side facing cast off 16 sts, patt to end (54 sts).

Row 8 patt to last 3 sts, p2 tog, p1.

Row 9 k1, k2 tog, patt to end (52 sts).

Rep the last 2 rows until 44 sts rem, then work straight until 8 panels (from the beginning) have been worked. Slip these 44 sts onto a st holder for right front shoulder. Return to rem 294 sts, slip next 42 sts onto a st holder for underarm, patt 140 sts, then turn. Work straight on these sts until 7 panels and 18 rows have been worked from the beginning.

Row 19 patt 47 sts, k2 tog, k1, turn.

Row 20 p1, p2 tog, patt to end.

Row 21 patt to last 3 sts, k2 tog, k1.

Rep the last 2 rows until 44 sts rem, then work straight until 8 panels have been worked from the beginning. Slip sts onto a st holder for right back shoulder. With right side facing slip next 40 sts onto a st holder for back neck, then work rem 50 sts as follows:

Row 19 patt to end.

Row 20 patt to last 3 sts, p2 tog, p1.

Row 21 k1, k2 tog, patt to end.

Rep the last 2 rows until 44 sts rem, then work straight until 8 panels have been worked from the beginning. Slip sts onto a st holder for left back shoulder. With right

side facing return to rem 112 sts, slip next 42 sts onto a st holder for underarm, then work straight on rem 70 sts until 7 panels and 7 rows have been worked from the beginning.

Row 8 cast off 16 sts, patt to end (wrong side facing).

Row 9 patt to last 3 sts, k2 tog, k1.

Row 10 p1, p2 tog, patt to end.

Rep the last 2 rows until 44 sts rem, then work straight until 8 panels have been worked from the beginning. Leave sts on needles for left front shoulder.

Shoulder seams
Graft (see page 155) right front shoulder to right back shoulder (right sides together). Rep for left shoulder. Block (see page 155) garment and press carefully on wrong side using a damp cloth.

Finishing pockets
Slip the 42 sts on st holder on right front onto 2¼ mm (size 13) needle and beginning with st 1, row 5, and decreasing 2 sts across 1st row, work 12 rows from chart B.

Rows 13 and 14 k in A (to make foldline).

Rows 15–26 as chart B, then cast off loosely. Rep for left front, but begin with st 5, row 5. Fold pocket tops to inside along foldline and stitch down neatly. Stitch pocket linings in place carefully on wrong side. Fold welt to inside along foldline and stitch down neatly. Weave in any loose ends using a darning needle (do not just cut them off).

SLEEVES
Remember all rounds are k and work chart A in rev order, from round 28–1.

With 3¼ mm (size 10) circular needle and A, slip the 42 sts from st holder onto needle and k in A, then pick up and k 118 sts around armhole (160 sts). Work 5 complete panels as chart A.

Change to set of 4 double-pointed 2¼ mm (size 13) needles.

Dec round 1 *k2 tog; rep from * to end (80 sts).

Dec round 2 *k8, k2 tog; rep from * to end (72 sts). Work 40 rounds as chart B.

Next round k in A.

Next round p in A (to make foldline), then work 40 more rounds as chart B and cast off loosely. Rep for 2nd sleeve.

Weave in any loose ends using a darning needle and then block (see page 155) and press on wrong side using a damp cloth. Fold cuffs to inside along foldline and stitch down neatly.

NECKBAND
With right side facing and 2¼ mm (size 13) needles and A, pick up and k 38 sts up right front to holder. K 40 sts from st holder, then pick up and k 38 sts down left front (116 sts).

Row 1 p.

Rows 2–13 as chart B, beginning at st 1, row 5, and

working 12 rows in patt.

Rows 14 and 15 k in A (to make foldline).

Rows 16–27 as chart B, then cast off loosely. Fold band to inside along foldline and stitch down neatly.

BUTTONHOLE BAND
With right side facing and 2¼ mm (size 13) needles and A, pick up and k 192 sts up right front edge between and not including welt and neckband.

Next row p in A, then cut off A.

Row 1 maintaining colour sequence of checks on welt, pick up and k 32 sts up side of welt, patt the 192 sts and then pick up and k 12 sts up edge of neckband (236 sts).

Rows 2–5 work from chart B, then make buttonholes.

Row 6 patt 4, *cast off 7, patt 30 (counting st already on needle); rep from * to last 10 sts, cast off 7, patt 3 (7 buttonholes).

Row 7 patt, casting on 7 sts over the 7 buttonholes.

Rows 8–12 work as chart B.

Rows 13 and 14 k in A.

Rows 15–19 work as chart B.

Rows 20 and 21 as rows 6 and 7.

Rows 22–26 work from chart B then cast off loosely. Fold band to inside along foldline and stitch down neatly. Neaten around buttonhole using small buttonhole st.

BUTTONBAND
With right side facing and 2¼ mm (size 13) needles and A, pick up and k 192 sts down left front edge between and not including neckband and welt.

Next row p in A, then cut off A.

Row 1 maintaining colour sequence of checks on neckband, pick up and k 12 sts down edge of neckband, patt the 192 sts and then pick up and k 32 sts down side of welt (236 sts).

Rows 2–12 work as chart B.

Rows 13 and 14 k in A.

Rows 15–26 work as chart B, then cast off loosely. Fold band to inside along foldline and stitch down neatly. Sew on buttons.

ARMHOLE FRILL
With set of 4 double-pointed 2¼ mm (size 13) needles and A, pick up and k 120 sts around top of right sleeve, beg at right back, not including underarm, then work 2 rows in k1 p1 rib.

Next row inc into every st (240 sts). Work rows 5–8 from chart B. K next 2 rows in D (to make foldline), then repeat rows 5–8 as chart B. Cast off. Fold frill at foldline and slip st into place. Rep for other armhole, beg picking up sts at left front.

HARLEQUIN

Many painters have been drawn to the world of the music hall and circus, to the clown, pierrot and acrobat. Picasso was particularly fond of the harlequin, whose sense of mischief and bespangled tights won Columbine's heart and made him so popular in pantomime. I have tried to echo that in my design. The scarlets and yellows are bright and bold. Greens act as borders and divide the panels and checks. The collar, cuffs and peplum are meant to add to its exuberance and sense of theatre.

MATERIALS
Pair of 2¼ mm (size 13) needles
Set of 4 double-pointed 2¼ mm (size 13) needles
Pair of 3¼ mm (size 10) needles
3¼ mm (size 10) crochet hook
5 buttons

WEIGHT OF YARN AND COLOURS
Scarlet (A)   280 g (10 oz)
Blue green (B)   230 g (8 oz)
Burgundy (C1)   57 g (2 oz)
Elderberry (C2)   57 g (2 oz)
Pale elderberry (C3)   57 g (2 oz)
Yellow (D1)   57 g (2 oz)
Buttercup yellow (D2)   57 g (2 oz)
Primrose (D3)   57 g (2 oz)

MEASUREMENTS
Length from top of shoulder to top of peplum: 44 cm (17½ in)
Actual width all round at underarm: 112 cm (44 in)
Sleeve length (excluding frill): 46 cm (18 in)

CHART A

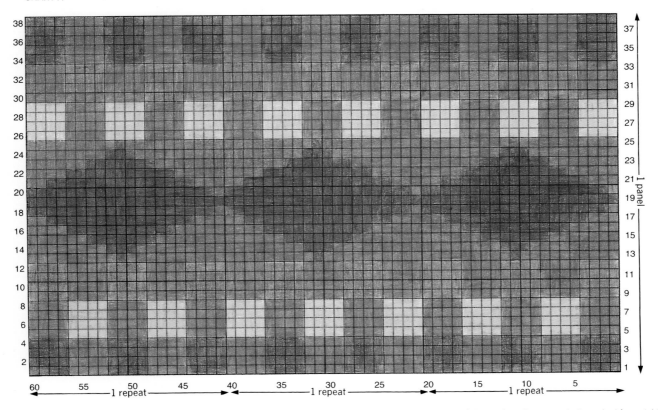

Odd-numbered rows are knit, worked from right to left.
Even-numbered rows are purl, worked from left to right.

TENSION

Over pattern, using 3¼ mm (size 10) needles, 26 sts and 30 rows to 10 cm (4 in).

IMPORTANT

● Twist wools at back of work every 1–2 sts to avoid making holes, but do not pull tight.
● When working st st using just one colour twist a spare ball of the same colour yarn across the back of work to keep the thickness of the garment even.
● Change shade of diamond motif every 2–3 rows to give a random effect.
● Work checks in one colour at a time, but vary which colour you use from panel to panel, especially for the collar, cuffs and peplum.
● This garment is knitted sideways, beginning at the left front edge, and the sleeves are also knitted sideways.
● The fronts and back and sleeves are worked from 2 charts – A and B – alternately, so check that you are referring to the correct chart each time you start a new panel.

INSTRUCTIONS
FRONTS AND BACK
Panel 1

With 3¼ mm (size 10) needles and A, cast on 84 sts and work from chart A, beg at st 1, row 13, working diamonds in C1, 2 and 3 in random numbers of rows.
Rows 13–20 as chart.
Cont working from chart, beg with right side row inc alternate rows to shape neck as follows:
Rows 21 and 23 patt to end, inc into last st.
Rows 25 and 27 patt to end, cast on 2 sts.
Rows 29 and 31 patt to end, cast on 3 sts.
Rows 33 and 35 patt to end, cast on 5 sts (106 sts).
Rows 36–38 as chart, then join on B and work 4 rows rev st st as follows.
Row 1 k.
Row 2 k.
Row 3 p.
Row 4 k.

Panel 2

Join on A and work from chart B, beg at st 1, row 1.

Rows 1–37 as chart.
Row 38 With wrong side facing cast off 52 sts (neck edge), patt to end (54 sts). Join on B and work 4 rows rev st st as before.

Panel 3 (underarm panel)

Join on A and work from chart A, beg at st 1, row 1.
Rows 1–38 as chart. Join on B and work 4 rows rev st st as before.

Panel 4

Join on A and work from chart B, beg at st 1, row 1.
Row 1 patt to end, cast on 52 sts (106 sts).
Rows 2–38 as chart. Join on B and work 4 rows rev st st as before.

Panel 5

Join on A and work from chart A, beg at st 1, row 1.
Rows 1–4 as chart.
Rows 5–11 dec 1 st at end (neck edge) of next and following 3 alternate rows (102 sts).
Rows 12–27 as chart.

CHART B

Odd-numbered rows are knit, worked from right to left.
Even-numbered rows are purl, worked from left to right.

Rows 28–34 inc 1 st at beg (neck edge) of next and following 3 alternate rows (106 sts).
Rows 35–38 as chart. Join on B and work 4 rows rev st st as before.

Panel 6

Join on A and work from chart B, beg at st 1, row 1.
Rows 1–37 as chart.
Row 38 cast off 52 sts (neck edge), patt to end (54 sts).
Join on B and work 4 rows rev st st as before.

Panel 7 (underarm panel)

Join on A and work from chart A, beg at st 1, row 1.
Rows 1–38 as chart. Join on B and work 4 rows rev st st as before.

Panel 8

Join on A and work from chart B, beg at st 1, row 1.
Row 1 patt to end, cast on 52 sts (106 sts).
Rows 2–38 as chart. Join on B and work 4 rows rev st st as before.

Panel 9

Join on A and work from chart A, beg at st 1, row 1.
Rows 1–3 as chart.
Cont working from chart, dec alternate rows as follows:
Rows 4 and 6 cast off 5 sts (neck edge), patt to end.
Rows 8 and 10 cast off 3 sts (neck edge), patt to end.
Rows 12 and 14 cast off 2 sts (neck edge), patt to end.

Rows 16 and 18 cast off 1 st (neck edge), patt to end (84 sts).
Rows 19–25 as chart.
Row 26 p using A only then cast off loosely in A.
Weave in any loose ends using a darning needle (do not just cut them off). Block (see page 155) garment and press carefully on wrong side using a damp cloth.

Shoulder seams

With right side facing and 2¼ mm (size 13) needles and B, pick up and k 40 sts along right front shoulder and work 4 rows rev st st as follows:
Row 1 k.
Row 2 p.
Row 3 k.
Row 4 p. Leave sts on a spare needle for grafting.
With right side facing and 2¼ mm (size 13) needles and B, pick up and k 40 sts along right back shoulder. Leave sts on needle. Graft (see page 155) right front shoulder to right back shoulder (right sides together). Rep for left shoulder.

SLEEVES

With 3¼ mm (size 10) needles and A, cast on 111 sts.
Work 6 complete panels from charts in order A, B, A, B, A and B. Work 4 rows rev st st in B between each panel and end with 4 rows rev st st in B. Leave sts on needle. Press carefully on wrong side using a damp cloth. Graft (see page 155) sts on needle to sts of cast on edge

(right sides together). Weave in any loose ends using a darning needle (do not just cut them off). Rep for 2nd sleeve.

Cuffs

With right side facing, ensuring patt is right way up, and set of 4 double-pointed 2¼ mm (size 13) needles and B, pick up and k 160 sts along lower edge of sleeve.
Round 1 *p2 tog; rep from * to end (80 sts).
Round 2 *p2, p2 tog; rep from * to end (60 sts).
Round 3 p.
Round 4 k.
Rounds 5–7 p.
Round 8 k.
Rounds 9–11 p.
Round 12 k.
Rounds 13–15 p.
Round 16 k, then cast off loosely.
Frill With 3¼ mm (size 10) needles and B, cast on 20 sts and k 2 rows. Join on A and work from chart C, shaping as follows:
Row 1 k.
Row 2 p 19 sts, turn.
Row 3 k.
Row 4 p 18 sts, turn.
Row 5 k.
Row 6 p 17 sts, turn.
Row 7 k to end.
Row 8 p to end.

Rows 9 and 10 join on B and k across all sts.
Rep these 10 rows as chart C until 16 panels have been worked, ending panel 16 with row 8. Keep sts on needle. Then, graft (see page 155) sts on needle to cast on edge (right sides together).
With set of 4 double-pointed 2¼ mm (size 13) needles and B, pick up and k 120 sts along shaped edge of Frill.
Dec round *k2 tog; rep from * to end (60 sts), then cast off loosely.
Stitch this edge of Frill to cast off edge of Cuff using small back sts (right sides tog). Rep for 2nd sleeve.

WELT

With right side facing and 2¼ mm (size 13) needles and B, pick up and k 170 sts along lower edge of fronts and back.
Row 1 k.
Row 2 p.
Rows 3–5 k.
Row 6 p.
Rows 7 and 8 k.
Rep rows 1–8 once and keep sts on needle.

PEPLUM

With 3¼ mm (size 10) needles and A, cast on 36 sts and work from chart C, shaping as follows:
Row 1 k.
Row 2 p 35 sts, turn.
Row 3 k.
Row 4 p 34 sts, turn.
Row 5 k.
Row 6 p 33 sts, turn.
Row 7 k to end.
Row 8 p to end.

Rows 9 and 10 join on B and k across all sts.
Rep these 10 rows as chart C until 57 panels have been worked, ending panel 57 with row 8, then cast off loosely.
With right side facing and 2¼ mm (size 13) needles and B, pick up and k 340 sts along shaped edge of Peplum.
Dec row *k2 tog; rep from * to end (170 sts). Keep sts on needle and graft (see page 155) them to sts on needle for Welt (right sides together).

NECKBAND

With wrong side facing and 2¼ mm (size 13) needles and B, pick up and k 87 sts along neck edge, beg at left front edge. Work 4 rows rev st st as follows:
Row 1 k.
Row 2 p.
Row 3 k.
Row 4 p. Leave sts on needle.

COLLAR

With 3¼ mm (size 10) needles and A, cast on 28 sts and work from chart C, shaping as follows:
Row 1 k.
Row 2 p 27 sts, turn.
Row 3 k.
Row 4 p 26 sts, turn.
Row 5 k.
Row 6 p 25 sts, turn.
Row 7 k.
Row 8 p.
Rows 9 and 10 join on B and k.
Rep these 10 rows as chart C until 29 panels have been worked, ending panel 29 with row 8, then cast off loosely.

With right side facing and 2¼ mm (size 13) needles and B, pick up and k 174 sts along shaped edge of Collar.
Dec row *k2 tog; rep from * to end (87 sts). Keep sts on needle and graft (see page 155) them to sts of Neckband.

BUTTONHOLE BAND

With right side facing and 2¼ mm (size 13) needles and B, pick up and k 100 sts up right front edge, beg at lower edge of Welt.
Row 1 k.
Row 2 p.
Rows 3–5 k, then make buttonholes.
Row 6 p3, cast off 6 sts, *p16 (including st on right-hand needle), cast off 6; rep from * to last 3 sts, p3.
Row 7 k, casting on 6 sts over the 5 buttonholes.
Rows 8 and 9 k.
Row 10 p.
Rows 11–13 k.
Row 14 p.
Rows 15–17 k.
Rows 18 and 19 as rows 6 and 7.
Rows 20 and 21 k.
Row 22 p.
Row 23 k, then cast off loosely purlwise.
Fold band to inside and stitch down neatly, neatening around buttonholes using a small buttonhole st.

BUTTONBAND

With right side facing and 2¼ mm (size 13) needles and B, pick and k 100 sts down left front edge to lower edge of Welt. K 1 row, p 1 row, k 3 rows, p 1 row, k 3 rows, p 1 row, k 3 rows, p 1 row, k 3 rows, p 1 row, k 3 rows, p 1 row, k 1 row, then cast off loosely purlwise. Fold band to inside and stitch down neatly. Sew on buttons.

SLEEVE INSERTION

Make 4 pleats – 2 each side of centre panel, 2 facing front and 2 facing back – as follows. With panel 4 as centre panel, take left-hand edge of panel 4 – folding along left-hand edge of rev st st – to centre of panel 3 and take left-hand edge of panel 3 – also folding along left-hand edge of rev st st – to centre of panel 2, then take right-hand edge of panel 4 – folding along right-hand edge of rev st st – to centre of panel 5 and take right-hand edge of panel 5 – also folding along right-hand edge of rev st st – to centre of panel 6. Stitch pleats down neatly.
With right side facing and set of 4 double-pointed 2¼ mm (size 13) needles and B, pick up and k 132 sts along top edge of sleeve. Work 4 rounds in p and keep sts on needles.
Place sleeve in armhole (right sides tog) and match panel 1 with underarm panel of fronts and back and centre of panel 4 with shoulder seam. Graft (see page 155) sts of sleeve to sts of armhole. Rep for 2nd sleeve.
With 3¼ mm (size 10) crochet hook and B, work 2 rows double crochet (see page 155) along edges of Collar, Cuff frills and Peplum.

CHART C

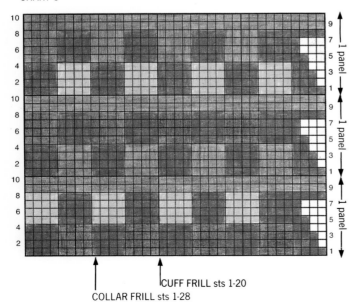

CUFF FRILL sts 1-20
COLLAR FRILL sts 1-28

PATCHWORK FANS

Two of my knitters are sisters in their seventies who both adore knitting. They laugh a lot as well, which makes visiting them a delight. One knits the most perfect Fair Isle cardigans I have ever seen, but the other can only knit plain jerseys. This design was the result of trying to create something specially for her. The knitting has a patchwork effect and the fans are knitted separately and appliquéed on afterwards, using the traditional Dorset feather stitch. The dyeing is made quicker if all the navy is done in one go, and the fans can be in any colour combination you like. It's a good jersey for using up leftover yarn.

MATERIALS

Pair of 2¼ mm (size 13) needles
Set of 4 double-pointed 2¼ mm (size 13) needles
Pair of 3¼ mm (size 10) needles
Circular 3¼ mm (size 10) needles 40 cm (16 in) long
6 stitch holders
6 buttons

WEIGHT OF YARN AND COLOURS

Navy (A)   460 g (16 oz)
Natural (B)   85 g (3 oz)
Red (C)   85 g (3 oz)
Dark Indigo blue (D)   85 g (3 oz)

MEASUREMENTS

Length from top of shoulder to bottom edge of cardigan: 53.5 cm (21 in)
Actual width all round at underarm: 122 cm (48 in)
Sleeve length: 51 cm (20 in)

TENSION

Over double moss stitch, using 3¼ mm (size 10) needles, 26 stitches and 32 rows to 10 cm (4 in).

IMPORTANT

● The fans are knitted separately and appliquéed on afterwards.
● The sleeves are knitted from shoulder to cuff.
● As the sleeves are worked on circular needles all stitches are knit unless otherwise stated.

INSTRUCTIONS
FRONTS AND BACK

With 2¼ mm (size 13) needles and A, cast on 280 sts and work 43 rows in k1 p1 rib.

Inc row *rib 13, inc into next st; rep from * to end (300 sts). Change to 3¼ mm (size 10) needles and patt (right side facing) as follows:

Row 1 *[k2 p2] 7 times, k2, p30; rep from * to end.
Row 2 *k30, [p2 k2] 7 times, p2; rep from * to end.
Row 3 *[p2 k2] 7 times, p2, p30; rep from * to end.
Row 4 *k30, [k2 p2] 7 times, k2; rep from * to end.
Rows 5–34 rep these 4 rows 7 times then rows 1–2 once.
Row 35 *p30, [k2 p2] 7 times, k2; rep from * to end.
Row 36 *[p2 k2] 7 times, p2, k30; rep from * to end.
Row 37 *p30, [k2 p2] 7 times p2; rep from * to end.
Row 38 *[k2 p2] 7 times, k2, k30; rep from * to end.
Rows 39–68 rep rows 35–38 7 times and then rows 35–36 once.
These 68 rows form patt.
Cont in patt, working rows 1–20 again.

Divide for fronts and back

Row 21 With right side facing patt 56 sts, turn and leave rem sts on a spare needle. Cont in patt on these 56 sts for right front until row 68 has been worked, ending at front edge.

Neck shaping

Row 1 With right side facing cast off 12 sts, patt to end.
Rows 2–9 cont in patt, dec 1 st at neck edge every row (36 sts).
Rows 10–16 work in patt, then slip sts onto a st holder for shoulder grafting.

Return to rem 244 sts on spare needle. With right side facing slip next 38 sts onto a st holder for right underarm and patt 112 sts (row 21), turn.
Row 22 cont in patt on these 112 sts until row 68 has been worked. Then work rows 1–12 of patt.
Rows 13–16 With right side facing patt 38 sts, k2 tog, turn, then dec 1 st at this edge (neck edge) on next 3 rows (36 sts).
Row 17 patt, then slip sts onto a st holder for shoulder grafting. Slip next 32 sts onto a st holder for back neck, then return to rem 40 sts, k2 tog, then patt (row 13) to end (39 sts).
Row 14 patt to last 2 sts, k2 tog (neck edge).
Rows 15 and 16 dec 1 st at neck edge (36 sts).
Row 17 patt, then slip sts onto a st holder for shoulder grafting. Return to rem 94 sts and with right side facing slip next 38 sts onto a st holder for left underarm, then patt to end (56 sts). Cont in patt until row 68 has been worked.
Row 1 With right side facing patt to end.
Row 2 With wrong side facing cast off 12 sts, patt to end.
Rows 3–10 dec 1 st at neck edge every row (36 sts).
Rows 11–16 patt, then leave sts on needle for shoulder.

SHOULDER SEAMS

Graft (see page 155) right front shoulder to right back shoulder (right sides together). Rep for left shoulder.

SLEEVES

With right side facing and 3¼ mm (size 10) circular needle, work 38 sts on st holder for first armhole as follows: k3, *k2 tog, k2; rep from * to last 3 sts, k3 (30 sts). Then pick up and k 90 sts around armhole (120 sts). For right sleeve, beg at round 1 of patt (m st) and for left sleeve, beg at round 35 of patt (rev st st) as sleeve and body patches at underarm and patches at shoulder will then match. Work 136 rounds in patt as below:

Rounds 1–2 *[k2, p2] 7 times, k2, p30; rep from * to end of round.
Rounds 3–4 *[p2, k2] 7 times, p2, p30; rep from * to end of round.
Rounds 5–34 Rep these 4 rounds 7 times and rounds 1–2 again.
Rounds 35–36 *p30, [k2, p2] 7 times, k2; rep from * to end of round.
Rounds 37–38 *p30, [p2, k2] 7 times, p2; rep from * to end of round.
Rounds 39–68 Rep rounds 35–38 7 times and rounds 35–36 again.
Change to set of 4 double-pointed 2¼ mm (size 13) needles.
Dec round 1 *p2, p2 tog; rep from * to end (90 sts).
Dec round 2 *p1, p2 tog; rep from * to end (60 sts).

Cuffs

Work 45 rounds in k1 p1 rib. Join on 2nd strand and using yarn double cast off loosely in rib. Weave in any loose ends using a darning needle (do not just cut them off). Block (see page 155) garment and press carefully on wrong side using a damp cloth, but do not press ribbing.

NECKBAND

With right side facing and 2¼ mm (size 13) needles, pick up and k 39 sts from right front neck edge to st holder. Then k 32 sts from st holder and pick up and k 39 sts to left front neck edge (110 sts). Work 9 rows in k1 p1 rib. Next row p (to make foldline), then work 9 more rows in k1 p1 rib. Cast off loosely in rib. Fold band to inside along foldline and stitch down neatly.

BUTTONHOLE BAND

With right side facing and 2¼ mm (size 13) needles, pick up and k 162 sts up right front edge.
Rows 1–4 work in k1 p1 rib, then make buttonholes.
Row 5 rib 3, cast off 6 sts, *rib 24 (counting st already on needle), cast off 6 sts; rep from * to last 3 sts, rib 3.
Row 6 cont in k1 p1 rib, casting on 6 sts over the 6 buttonholes.
Rows 7–9 work in k1 p1 rib.
Row 10 p (to make foldline).
Rows 11–13 work in k1 p1 rib.

Rows 14 and 15 as rows 5 and 6.
Rows 16–19 work in k1 p1 rib, then cast off loosely in rib. Fold band to inside along foldline and stitch down neatly, neatening around buttonholes using a small buttonhole st.

BUTTONBAND

With right side facing and 2¼ mm (size 13) needles, pick up and k 162 sts down left front edge. Work 9 rows in k1 p1 rib, p next row (to make foldline), work 9 more rows in k1 p1 rib, then cast off loosely in rib. Fold band to inside along foldline and stitch down. Sew on buttons.

FANS

With 2¼ mm (size 13) needles and C, cast on 22 sts.
Row 1 k.
Row 2 p19, turn.
Row 3 k.
Row 4 p12, turn.
Row 5 k.
Row 6 p5, turn.
Row 7 k.
Row 8 p21, slip 1.
Rows 1–8 form one section of fan. Rep rows 1–8 7 more times, making 7 more sections using colours in following order: B, D, B, C, B, D, B, then cast off. Make 35 more fans. Place a fan in each rev st st square, all facing the same way. With a darning needle and strand of B, slip st bottom of fan into place using small, neat sts. With strand of C, sew vertical edge of fan into place. With strand of D, feather st top edge of fan (see below). With strand of D, sew 5 small rows of chain st (see page 157) from bottom edge of fan into corner of rev st st square (see picture above). Rep for each fan.

FEATHER STITCH

This is worked from top to bottom. Bring the needle up through the work, where you want the centreline of the stitches to be. Insert the needle at a point slightly lower and to the left, and slant it to the right, so that you can bring it out on the centreline with the thread looped *under* the point of the needle. Next insert the needle slightly lower and to the right this time and, slanting it to the left, make a similar looped stitch. Continue, alternating the stitches from left to right, keeping them evenly spaced.

BELLS AND CHECKS

I have always loved the attention to detail in Elizabethan costume – the way bows, pleating and embroidery transformed a commonplace garment into something out of the ordinary. On this jacket every panel has a different colour and pattern combination, and the pleated sleeves are deliberately grafted onto the body so they don't match, making it random and theatrical. Weave the wool on every stitch and pay as much attention to the inside of the jacket as the outside.

MATERIALS

Pair of 2¼ mm (size 13) needles
Set of 4 double-pointed 2¼ mm (size 13) needles
Pair of 3¼ mm (size 10) needles
7 buttons

WEIGHT OF YARN AND COLOURS

Dark Indigo blue (A)   230 g (8 oz)
Crimson (B)   280 g (10 oz)
Navy (C)   340 g (12 oz)
Natural (D)   170 g (6 oz)

MEASUREMENTS

Length from top of shoulder to bottom edge of cardigan: 61 cm (24 in)
Actual width all round at underarm: 147 cm (58 in)
Sleeve length: 51 cm (20 in)

TENSION

Over pattern, using 3¼ mm (size 10) needles, 30 stitches and 30 rows to 10 cm (4 in).

IMPORTANT

- Twist wools at back of work every 1–2 stitches to avoid making holes, but do not pull tight.
- When working st st using just one colour twist a spare ball of the same colour yarn across the back of work to keep the thickness of the garment even.
- This garment is knitted sideways, beginning at the left front edge, and the sleeves are also knitted sideways.
- Before beginning each new panel, check with the diagram below to ensure that you have the correct colour combination.

Key
S = background A, flower B, stem C
T = checks in B and D
U = background B, flower C, stem D
V = checks in B and C
W = background C, flower D, stem B
X = checks in A and D
Y = checks in A and B
Z = checks in C and D

INSTRUCTIONS
FRONTS AND BACK

Panel 1

With 3¼ mm (size 10) needles and colour combination S, cast on 126 sts in A and work from chart A, beginning at st 1, row 1.
Rows 1–12 as chart.

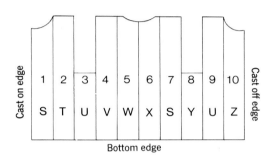

Bottom edge

Neck shaping

Row 13 With right side facing inc 1 st at end (neck edge) of row.
Rows 14–16 as chart.
Rows 17–29 inc 1 st at end (neck edge) of this and next 6 alternate rows (134 sts).
Rows 30–31 as chart.
Row 32 With wrong side facing cast on 15 sts (neck edge), patt to end (149 sts).
Rows 33–42 as chart, then work 4 rows rev st st in C as follows:
Row 1 k.
Row 2 k.
Row 3 p.
Row 4 k.

Panel 2

Using colour combination T, work from chart B, beginning at st 1, row 1.
Rows 1–41 as chart.
Row 42 With wrong side facing cast off 52 sts (neck edge), patt to end (97 sts), then work 4 rows rev st st in C as before.

Odd-numbered rows are knit, worked from right to left.
Even-numbered rows are purl, worked from left to right.

CHART A

1 repeat

CHART B

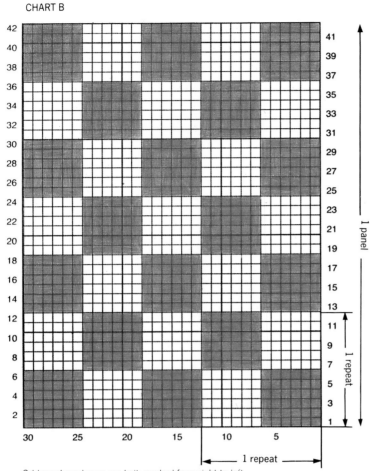

Odd-numbered rows are knit, worked from right to left.
Even-numbered rows are purl, worked from left to right.

Panel 10
Using colour combination Z, work from chart B.
Rows 1–11 as chart.
Neck shaping
Row 12 With wrong side facing cast off 15 sts, patt to end (134 sts).
Rows 13–14 as chart.
Rows 15–27 dec 1 st at end (neck edge) of this and next 6 alternate rows (127 sts).
Rows 28–30 as chart.
Row 31 dec 1 st at end (neck edge) of row (126 sts).
Rows 32–42 as chart, then cast off loosely. Weave in any loose ends with a darning needle (do not just cut them off). Block (see page 155) garment and press carefully on wrong side using a damp cloth.

Shoulder seams
With right side facing and 2¼ mm (size 13) needles and C, pick up and k 52 sts along right front shoulder. K 1 row, p 1 row and k 1 row. Leave sts on a spare needle. With 2¼ mm (size 13) needles and C, pick up and k 52 sts along right back shoulder and leave sts on needle. Graft (see page 155) right front shoulder to right back shoulder (right sides together). Rep for left shoulder.

SLEEVES
Left sleeve
With 3¼ mm (size 10) needles and A, cast on 123 sts.
Work 6 complete panels with 4 rows rev st st in C between each panel with colour combinations in following order:
Panel 1 (underarm panel) Y.
Panel 2 U.
Panel 3 Z.
Panel 4 W.
Panel 5 X.
Panel 6 S.
Then work 4 rows rev st st in C and keep sts on needle. Weave in any loose ends using a darning needle (do not just cut them off). Press carefully on wrong side using a damp cloth, then graft (see page 155) sts on needle to cast on edge (right sides together).

Right sleeve
Work as Left sleeve but in following colour combinations:
Panel 1 (underarm panel) W.
Panel 2 X.
Panel 3 S.
Panel 4 T.
Panel 5 U.
Panel 6 V.

Panel 3 (underarm panel)
Using colour combination U, work from chart A.
Rows 1–42 as chart, then work 4 rows rev st st in C as before.

Panel 4
Using colour combination V, work from chart B.
Row 1 With right side facing patt to end of row (neck edge) then cast on 52 sts (149 sts).
Rows 2–42 as chart, then work 4 rows rev st st in C as before.

Panel 5
Using colour combination W, work from chart A.
Rows 1–10 as chart.
Rows 11–15 dec 1 st at end (neck edge) of this and next 2 alternate rows (146 sts).
Rows 16–42 as chart, then work 4 rows rev st st in C as before.

Panel 6
Using colour combination X, work from chart B.
Rows 1–26 as chart.

Rows 27–31 inc 1 st at end (neck edge) of this and next 2 alternate rows (149 sts).
Rows 32–42 as chart, then join on C and work 4 rows rev st st as before.

Panel 7
Using colour combination S, work from chart A
Rows 1–41 as chart.
Row 42 With wrong side facing cast off 52 sts (neck edge), patt to end (97 sts), then work 4 rows rev st st in C as before.

Panel 8 (underarm panel)
Using colour combination Y, work from chart B.
Rows 1–42 as chart, then join on C and work 4 rows rev st st as before.

Panel 9
Using colour combination U, work from chart A.
Row 1 With right side facing patt to end of row (neck edge) then cast on 52 sts (149 sts).
Rows 2–42 as chart, then work 4 rows rev st st in C as before.

Cuffs

With set of 4 double-pointed 2¼ mm (size 13) needles and C, pick up and k 160 sts around lower edge of sleeve (making sure patt is right way up and right side is facing). Loop short strand brightly coloured wool round 1st st of each round so that you can find beg of round easily.

Round 1 *k2 tog; rep from * to end (80 sts).
Round 2 *k2, k2 tog; rep from * to end (60 sts).
Join on 2nd strand C and using yarn double work 32 rounds in k1 p1 rib, then cast off loosely in rib.

WELT

With right side facing and 2¼ mm (size 13) needles and C, pick up and k 230 sts along lower edge of fronts and back. Join on 2nd strand C and using yarn double work 32 rows in k1 p1 rib. Cast off loosely in rib.

NECKBAND

With right side facing and 2¼ mm (size 13) needles and C, pick up and k 100 sts around neck, beg at right front neck edge. Join on 2nd strand C and using yarn double work 9 rows in k1 p1 rib, then cast off loosely in rib.

BUTTONHOLE BAND

With right side facing and 2¼ mm (size 13) needles and C, pick up and k 152 sts up right front edge.
Rows 1–4 join on 2nd strand C and using yarn double work in k1 p1 rib, then make buttonholes.
Row 5 rib 4, *cast off 6 sts, rib 17 (counting st already on needle) rep from * to last 10 sts, cast off 6 sts, rib 4.
Row 6 work in k1 p1 rib, casting on 6 sts over the 7 buttonholes.
Rows 7 and 8 work in k1 p1 rib, then cast off loosely in rib

BUTTONBAND

With right side facing and 2¼ mm (size 13) needles and C, pick up and k 152 sts down left front edge. Join on 2nd strand C and using yarn double work 8 rows in k1 p1 rib, then cast off loosely in rib. Sew on buttons.

SLEEVE INSERTION

Make 3 pleats in top of sleeve by folding rev st st edge of panel 4 to centre of panel 3, rev st st edge of panel 5 to centre of panel 4 and rev st st edge of panel 6 to centre of panel 5. Stitch the pleats down neatly (check that pleats face front of garment).
With set of 4 double-pointed 2¼ mm (size 13) needles and C, pick up and k 110 sts around top edge of sleeve (right side facing) and p 3 rounds. Leave sts on needle. Place sleeve in armhole (right sides together), matching underarm panel and middle pleat with shoulder seam, and graft (see page 155) tog. Weave in any rem loose ends using a darning needle (do not just cut them off).

CHEVRON

A few years ago my work was exhibited in Japan, which meant going out there to talk about it. I slipped away whenever I could, walking endlessly down narrow back streets in search of naturally dyed kimonos. Sadly, the ancient traditions of natural dyeing are virtually extinct, and the nearest I came to success was a tiny shop in Kyoto piled high with scraps of fabric. The old man who ran it spoke no English, and my Japanese is non-existent. Yet our love of textiles overcame the language barrier, and I eventually left with a small length of chevron-patterned kimono – the origin of this design. The triangles, squares and circles are geometric like the chevron, yet act as a contrast and foil. The box-pleated sleeves and centre back box pleat make the rest of the coat as much of a surprise as the front. Knit the variegated red colours randomly, and do the same with the elderberries.

MATERIALS

Pair of 2¼ mm (size 13) needles
2 pairs of 3¼ mm (size 10) needles
Circular 3¼ mm (size 10) needle 40 cm (16 in) long
Set of 4 double-pointed 3¼ mm (size 10) needles
3¼ mm (size 10) cable needle
2 stitch holders
7 buttons

WEIGHT OF YARN AND COLOURS

Navy (A)   450 g (16 oz)
Natural (B)   230 g (8 oz)
Blue green (C)   230 g (8 oz)
Scarlet (D1)   57 g (2 oz)
Crimson (D2)   57 g (2 oz)
Red (D3)   57 g (2 oz)
Medium Indigo blue (E)   230 g (8 oz)
Elderberry (F1)   57 g (2 oz)
Light Elderberry (F2)   57 g (2 oz)
Grape (F3)   57 g (2 oz)

MEASUREMENTS

Length from top of shoulder to bottom edge of coat:
90 cm (35½ in)
Actual width all round at underarm: 124 cm (49 in)
Sleeve length: 48 cm (19 in)

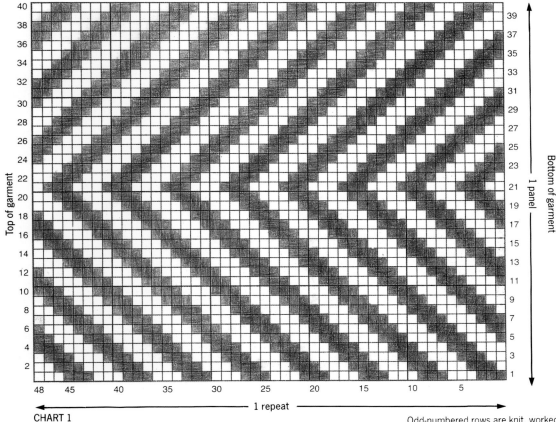

CHART 1

1 repeat

Top of garment

Bottom of garment

1 panel

Odd-numbered rows are knit, worked from right to left.
Even-numbered rows are purl, worked from left to right.

TENSION

Over pattern, using 3¼ mm (size 10) needles, 31 stitches and 30 rows to 10 cm (4 in).

IMPORTANT

● Twist wools at back of work every 1–2 stitches to avoid making holes, but do not pull tight.
● When working st st using just one colour twist a spare ball of the same colour yarn across the back of work to keep the thickness of the garment even.
● This garment is knitted sideways, beginning at the left front edge, and the sleeves are also knitted sideways.
● When using the circular needle, all rounds are knit.
● Change colours of shapes motifs every 2–3 rows to give a random effect.
● Chart 2 is worked in different colour combinations, so before beginning each new panel check that you have the correct colour combination: for the fronts and back, panels 2, 6 and 10 are in background colour C and the motif is in shades of D, panels 4 and 8 are in background colour E and the motif is in shades of F; for the sleeves, panels 2 and 6 are in background colour E and the motif is in F and panel 4 is in background colour C and the motif is in D.
● When working sleeves begin chart 1 at stitch 1, row 1, and chart 2 at stitch 26, row 1.

INSTRUCTIONS
FRONTS AND BACK
Panel 1

With 3¼ mm (size 10) needles and A, cast on 200 sts. Join on B and work from chart 1, beg at st 1, row 21.
Rows 1–6 (rows 21–26 of chart) as chart.
Cont working from chart, inc alternate rows as follows:
Row 7 with right side facing patt to end, then cast on 2 sts (neck edge).
Row 9 patt to end, cast on 2 sts (neck edge).
Row 11 patt to end, cast on 3 sts (neck edge).
Row 13 patt to end, cast on 3 sts (neck edge).
Row 15 patt to end, cast on 5 sts (neck edge).
Row 17 patt to end, cast on 5 sts (neck edge).
Row 19 patt to end, cast on 5 sts (neck edge; 225 sts).
Row 20 as chart, then join on 2nd strand A and work cable panel as follows.
Row 1 *k3, slip next 3 sts onto cable needle and leave at front of work, k 3 sts, then k 3 sts from cable needle; rep from * to end.
Rows 2–6 work in st st.
Row 7 as row 1.
Row 8 p.

Panel 2

Join on C and D and work from chart 2, beg at st 1, row 1.

Rows 1–31 as chart.
Pocket lining Lay work on one side and with 2nd pair of 3¼ mm (size 10) needles and C and D, cast on 60 sts and work rows 1–31 of chart 2, beg at st 30, row 1. Keep sts on spare needle.
Return to main body of work and cont as follows:
Row 32 with wrong side facing cast off 56 sts, patt 80 (including st on needle). Slip next 46 sts onto a st holder, then join on Pocket lining, p 1st 46 sts from its needle, then purl together last 14 sts of Pocket lining and next 14 sts of left front and patt to end (169 sts). Then join on 2 strands A and work 8 rows of cable panel in A as before.

Panel 3 (underarm panel)

Join on B and work from chart 1, beg at st 1, row 1.
Rows 1–40 as chart, then join on 2nd strand A and work 8 rows of cable panel in A as before.

Panel 4

Join on E and F and work from chart 2, beg at st 1, row 1.
Row 1 With right side facing patt to end (neck edge) then, cast on 56 sts (225 sts).
Rows 2–32 as chart, then join on 2 strands A and work 8 rows of cable panel as before.

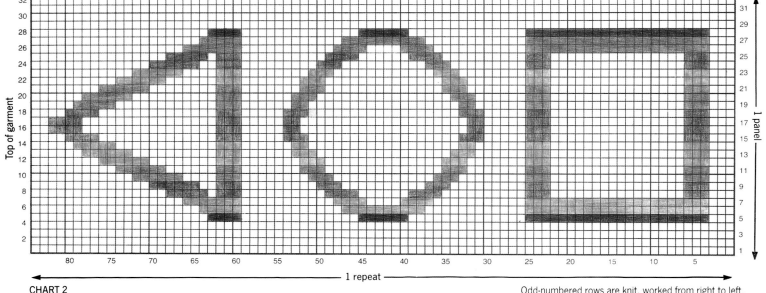

CHART 2

Odd-numbered rows are knit, worked from right to left.
Even-numbered rows are purl, worked from left to right.

Panel 5
Join on B and work from chart 1, beg at st 1, row 1.
Rows 1–40 as chart, then join on 2nd strand A and work 8 rows of cable panel as before.

Panel 6
Join on C and D and work from chart 2, beg at st 1, row 1.
Rows 1–32 as chart, then join on 2 strands A and work 8 rows of cable panel as before.

Panel 7
Join on B and work from chart 1, beg at st 1, row 1.
Rows 1–40 as chart, then join on 2nd strand A and work 8 rows of cable panel as before.

Panel 8
Join on E and F and work from chart 2, beg at st 1, row 1.
Rows 1–31 as chart.
Row 32 With wrong side facing cast off 56 sts, patt to end (169 sts), then join on 2 strands A and work 8 rows of cable panel as before.

Panel 9 (underarm panel)
Join on B and work from chart 1, beg at st 1, row 1.
Rows 1–40 as chart, then join on 2nd strand A and work 8 rows of cable panel as before.
Pocket top Lay work on one side and, with 3¼ mm (size 10) needles and 2 strands A, cast on 46 sts and work 8 rows of cable panel as before. Keep sts on spare needle.
Return to main body of work and cont as follows:

Panel 10
Join on C and D and work from chart 2, beg at st 1, row 1.
Row 1 With right side facing patt 43 sts, slip sts of Pocket top onto needle and k them. Slip next 46 sts onto a st holder, patt 80 sts, then turn and cast on 56 sts (225 sts).
Rows 2–32 as chart, then join on 2 strands A and work 8 rows of cable panel as before.

Panel 11
Join on B and work from chart 1, beg at st 1, row 1, dec alternate rows as follows:
Row 2 With wrong side facing cast off 5 sts, patt to end.
Row 4 cast off 5 sts (neck edge), patt to end.
Row 6 cast off 5 sts (neck edge), patt to end.
Row 8 cast off 3 sts (neck edge), patt to end.
Row 10 cast off 3 sts (neck edge), patt to end.
Row 12 cast off 2 sts (neck edge), patt to end.
Row 14 cast off 2 sts (neck edge), patt to end (200 sts).
Rows 15–20 as chart, then cast off loosely. Weave in any loose ends using a darning needle (do not just cut them off). Block (see page 155) garment and press carefully on wrong side using a damp cloth.

Finishing pockets
Left pocket top With wrong side facing and 3¼ mm (size 10) needles and C, slip the 46 sts from st holder onto needle and p them. Using 2 strands A, work 8 rows of cable panel as before then cast off loosely.
Right pocket lining With right side facing and 3¼ mm (size 10) needles and C and D, slip the 46 sts from st holder onto needle then with C cast on 14 sts (60 sts).

Work rows 1–32 as chart 2, then cast off loosely. Stitch Pocket linings in place carefully, stitching down the 14 sts cast on for Right pocket lining along 1st row of panel and stitch down edges of Pocket tops.

Shoulder seams
With right side facing and 3¼ mm (size 10) needles and A, pick up and k 42 sts along right front shoulder. Join on 2nd strand A and p 1 row, then work 8 rows of cable panel as before. Leave sts on a spare needle.
With 3¼ mm (size 10) needles and A, pick up and k 42 sts along right back shoulder and leave sts on needle. Graft (see page 155) right front shoulder to right back shoulder (right sides together). Rep for left shoulder.

SLEEVES
With 3¼ mm (size 10) needles and A, cast on 125 sts. Work 6 panels – working alternately from charts 1 and 2, beginning chart 1 at st 1, row 1, and chart 2 at st 26, row 1. Beg with chart 1, and work colour combinations for chart B as follows: panels 2 and 6 in E and F and panel 4 in C and D – work 8 rows of cable panel in 2 strands A between each panel as before and end with 8 rows of cable panel in A. Leave sts on needle. Press carefully on wrong side using a damp cloth.
Make a box pleat by folding panels 3 and 5 in half and bringing the folded edges tog at centre of panel 4. Stitch pleat down neatly at top and bottom edges of sleeve.

Cuffs
With right side facing and 2¼ mm (size 13) needles and A, pick up and k 160 sts along lower edge of sleeve.
Dec row 1 *k2 tog; rep from * to end (80 sts).

Dec row 2 *k2, k2 tog; rep from * to end (60 sts).
Rows 3–5 k.
Join on B and work from chart 1, beg at st 1, row 9.
Rows 9–33 work as chart. P 1 round with A.
Then k 6 rows, join on 2nd strand A and cast off loosely
purlwise.
Graft (see page 155) sts on needle to sts of cast on edge
(right sides together). Using a small back st and
matching chevrons, sew edges of cuff together.

WELT

Make a box pleat at centre back by folding panels 5 and
7 in half and bringing the folded edges tog at centre of
panel 6. Stitch pleat down neatly at top and bottom
edges. With right side facing and 2¼ mm (size 13)
needles and A, pick up and k 320 sts along lower edge
of fronts and back, ensuring that sts are picked up
through all layers of pleat. Join on 2nd strand A and k 5
rows. Then join on B. Turn chart upside down and,
beginning with a k row, work from row 40 back to row 1
to reverse direction of chevron. Break off B, k 8 rows
with A, then cast off loosely knitwise.

NECKBAND

With right side facing and 2¼ mm (size 13) needles and
A, pick up and k 120 sts around neck. K 5 rows, then
join on B and work rows 13–27 as chart 1. Break off B,
then, in A, p 1 row, k 4 rows. Join on 2nd strand A and
cast off loosely purlwise.

BUTTONHOLE BAND

With right side facing and 2¼ mm (size 13) needles and
A, pick up and k 200 sts up right front edge. Join on
2nd strand A.
Rows 1–3 k.
Row 4 k 4 sts, cast off 6, *k 25 (including st on needle),
cast off 6; rep from * to last 4 sts, k 4.
Row 5 k, casting on 6 sts over the 7 buttonholes.
Rows 6–8 k. Cast off loosely knitwise.

BUTTONBAND

With right side facing and 2¼ mm (size 13) needles and
A, pick up and k 200 sts down left front edge. Join on
2nd strand A and k 8 rows, then cast off loosely
knitwise. Sew on buttons.

SLEEVE INSERTION

Remember when using a circular needle, k every
round.
With right side facing and 3¼ mm (size 10) circular
needle and A, pick up and k 135 sts around top edge of
sleeve. Join on 2nd strand A and work 8 rounds of cable
panel, then cast off loosely.
With 3¼ mm (size 10) circular needle and A, pick up
and k 135 sts around armhole. Leave sts on needle and
graft (see page 155) to cast off edge of cable panel of
sleeve, matching underarm panels and pleat with centre
of cable panel at shoulder seam. Weave in any rem
loose ends using a darning needle (do not just cut off).

PINKS AND RIBBONS

Part of the pleasure of working with a team of knitters is that each person can suggest ideas which eventually become a design. In this case it was the ultimate romantic combination of ribbons and roses, but however much I drew it on graph paper the shape refused to balance. Then the roses became pinks, I joined the bows with a vertical ribbon, and suddenly the design fell into place. The ruffles are all picked up after the main bulk of the knitting is completed. The coat is both feminine and versatile, and can be worn with scruffy jeans or a silk evening dress. If you don't squeeze the wool too thoroughly when dyeing it in the indigo it will emerge as a multitude of uneven blues, making it more fun to knit and visually more exciting.

MATERIALS

Pair of 2¼ mm (size 13) needles
Set of 4 double-pointed 2¼ mm (size 13) needles
Circular 2¼ mm (size 13) needle
Pair of 3¼ mm (size 10) needles
Set of 4 double-pointed 3¼ mm (size 10) needles
Circular 3¼ mm (size 10) needle 80 cm (31½ in) long
  (optional)
6 buttons

WEIGHT OF YARN AND COLOURS

Grey (A)   170 g (6 oz)
Medium Indigo blue (B)   170 g (6 oz)
Dark Indigo blue (C)   115 g (4 oz)
Redwood pink (D1)   57 g (2 oz)
Crimson (D2)   57 g (2 oz)
Magenta (D3)   57 g (2 oz)
Red (D4)   57 g (2 oz)
Blue green (E)   115 g (4 oz)

CHART A

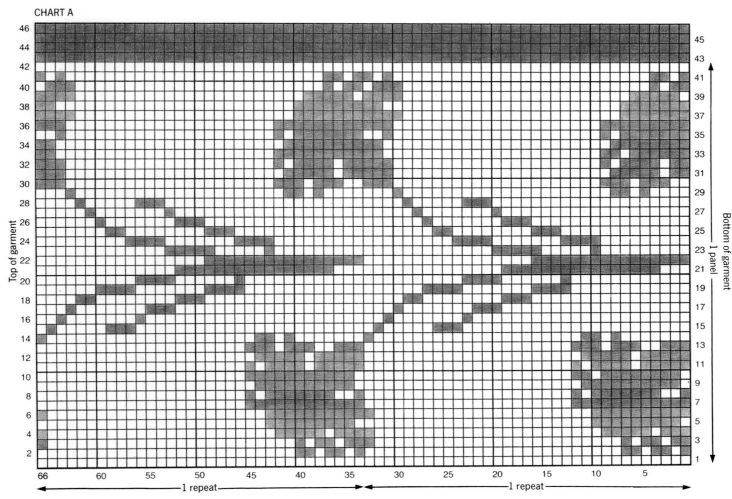

Even-numbered rows are purl, worked from left to right: Odd-numbered rows are knit, worked from right to left.

MEASUREMENTS

Length from top of shoulder to bottom edge of cardigan: 53.5 cm (21 in)
Actual width all round at underarm: 117 cm (46 in)
Sleeve length: 57 cm (22½ in)

TENSION

Over pattern, using 3¼ mm (size 10) needles, 30 sts and 32 rows to 10 cm (4 in).

IMPORTANT

● Change shade of red on pinks and ribbons motifs every 2–3 rows to give a random effect.
● Twist wools at back of work every 1–2 sts to avoid making holes, but do not pull tight.
● When working st st using just one colour twist a spare ball of the same colour yarn across the back of work to keep the thickness of the garment even.
● This garment is knitted sideways, beginning at the left front edge, and the sleeves are also knitted sideways.

● There are two background colours so always check that you are using the correct colour: panels 1, 3, 5, 7 and 9 are in A and panels 2, 4, 6 and 8 are in B.

INSTRUCTIONS
FRONTS AND BACK
Panel 1

With 3¼ mm (size 10) needles and A, cast on 104 sts.
K 1 row, p 1 row, then work 12 rows as chart A, beg at st 20, row 15.

Cont working from chart, and beg with a right side row inc alternate rows to shape neck as follows:
Rows 27 and 29 inc 1 st at end (neck edge) of row.
Rows 31 and 33 cast on 2 sts at end (neck edge) of row.
Rows 35 and 37 cast on 3 sts at end (neck edge) of row.
Rows 39 and 41 cast on 5 sts at end (neck edge) of row (126 sts).
Row 42 as chart. Work 4 rows rev st st in C as follows:
Row 1 k.
Row 2 k.
Row 3 p.
Row 4 k.

Panel 2

Join on B and work from chart B, beg at st 10, row 1.
Rows 1–41 as chart.
Row 42 With wrong side facing cast off 52 sts (neck edge), patt to end (74 sts).
Join on C and work 4 rows rev st st as before.

92 PINKS AND RIBBONS

CHART B

Odd-numbered rows are knit, worked from right to left.
Even-numbered rows are purl, worked from left to right.

Panel 3 (underarm panel)
Join on A and work from chart A, beg at st 20, row 1.
Rows 1–42 as chart. Join on C and work 4 rows rev st st as before.

Panel 4
Join on B and work from chart B, beg at st 10, row 1.
Row 1 Patt to end (neck edge); then cast on 52 sts (126 sts).
Rows 2–42 as chart, then join on C and work 4 rows rev st st as before.

Panel 5
Join on A and work from chart A, beg at st 20, row 1, dec 1 st at end (neck edge) of first and every following 4th row until 122 sts rem. Then work straight until row 29 of chart has been worked.
Row 30 inc 1 st at the beg (neck edge) of this and every following 4th row until there are 126 sts, then join on C and work 4 rows rev st st as before.

Panel 6
Join on B and work from chart B, beg at st 10, row 1.
Rows 1–41 as chart.
Row 42 cast off 52 sts (neck edge), patt to end (74 sts).
Join on C and work 4 rows rev st st as before.

Panel 7 (underarm panel)
Join on A and work from chart A, beg at st 20, row 1.
Rows 1–42 as chart. Join on C and work 4 rows rev st st as before.

Panel 8
Join on B and work from chart B, beg at st 10, row 1.
Row 1 Patt to end (neck edge) then cast on 52 sts (126 sts).
Rows 2–42 as chart. Join on C and work 4 rows rev st st as before.

Panel 9
Join on A and work from chart A, beg at st 20, row 1.
Row 1 as chart.
Cont working from chart, dec alternate rows as follows:
Rows 2 and 4 cast off 5 sts (neck edge), patt to end.
Rows 6 and 8 cast off 3 sts (neck edge), patt to end.
Rows 10 and 12 cast off 2 sts (neck edge), patt to end.
Rows 14 and 16 cast off 1 st (neck edge), patt to end (104 sts).
Rows 17–28 as chart. Using A, k 1 row and p 1 row. Cast off loosely. Weave in any loose ends using a darning needle (do not just cut them off). Block (see page 155) garment and press carefully on wrong side using a damp cloth.

Shoulder seams
With right side facing and 2¼ mm (size 13) needles and C, pick up and k 40 sts along right front shoulder, K 1 row, p 1 row and k 1 row. Leave sts on a spare needle for grafting.

With right side facing and 2¼ mm (size 13) needles and C, pick up and k 40 sts along right back shoulder and leave sts on needle for grafting. Graft (see page 155) right front shoulder to right back shoulder (right sides together). Rep for left shoulder.

SLEEVES

With 3¼ mm (size 10) needles and A, cast on 133 sts. Work 4 complete panels with 4 rows rev st st in C between each panel, beg with 4 rows rev st st, working from charts in following order:
Panel 1 (underarm panel) chart A, beg at st 22, row 1.
Panel 2 chart B, beg at st 8, row 1.
Panel 3 chart A, beg at st 22, row 1.
Panel 4 chart B, beg at st 8, row 1.
Keep sts on needle. Weave in any loose ends using a darning needle (do not just cut them off). Press carefully on wrong side using a damp cloth. Graft (see page 155) cast on edge of sleeve to sts on needle (right sides together).

Cuffs

With right side facing, ensuring patt is right way up, and set of 4 double-pointed 2¼ mm (size 13) needles and C, pick up and k 122 sts around lower edge of sleeve.
Round 1 *k2 tog; rep from * to end (61 sts).
Round 2 *k4, k2 tog; rep from * to last 7 sts, k4, k3 tog (50 sts). Work 24 rounds in k1 p1 rib, looping short strand brightly coloured wool round 1st and last st of round 24 as a marker. Then work 2 rounds in k1 p1 rib.
Frill 1 Change to set of 4 double-pointed 3¼ mm (size 10) needles and work 1 round, inc into every st (100 sts), then join on E.
Next round work 1 row in k1 p1 rib.
Next round p, then cast off loosely knitwise.
Frill 2 With set of 4 double-pointed 2¼ mm (size 13) needles and C, pick up and k 50 sts along round indicated by marker on inside of Cuff. Work 5 rounds in k1 p1 rib, then change to set of 4 double-pointed 3¼ mm (size 10) needles and work 1 round, inc into every st (100 sts). Join on A.
Next round work 1 round in k1 p1 rib.
Next round p, then cast off loosely knitwise.
Frill 3 With set of 4 double-pointed 2¼ mm (size 13) needles and C, pick up and k 50 sts along round indicated by marker on inside of Cuff (this is exactly the same place as for Frill 2). Work 9 rounds in k1 p1 rib, then change to set of 4 double-pointed 3¼ mm (size 10) needles and work 1 round, inc into every st (100 sts).
Next round Join on D and work 1 round in k1 p1 rib.
Next round p, then cast off loosely knitwise.

WELT

With right side facing and 2¼ mm (size 13) needles and C, pick up and k 230 sts along lower edge of fronts and back and work 24 rows in k1 p1 rib. Loop short strand brightly coloured wool round 1st and last sts of row 24 as markers.
Frill 1 Change to 3¼ mm (size 10) needles and work 1 row, inc into every st (460 sts). (Tip: slip sts onto 3¼ mm (size 10) circular needle as this will accommodate all the sts more comfortably and just k from it lengthwise.) Join on E.
Next row work 1 row in k1 p1 rib.
Next row with wrong side facing k 1 row, then cast off loosely purlwise.
Frill 2 With 2¼ mm (size 13) needles and C, pick up and k 230 sts along row indicated by markers on inside of Welt. Work 5 rows in k1 p1 rib then change to 3¼ mm (size 10) needles (or circular needle as before) and work 1 row, inc into every st (460 sts). Join on A.
Next row work 1 row in k1 p1 rib.
Next row k, then cast off loosely purlwise.
Frill 3 With 2¼ mm (size 13) needles and C, pick up and k 230 sts along row indicated by markers on inside of Welt (this is exactly the same place as for Frill 2). Work 9 rows in k1 p1 rib, then change to 3¼ mm (size 10) needles (or circular needle as before) and work 1 row, inc into every st (460 sts). Join on D.
Next row work 1 row in k1 p1 rib.
Next row k, then cast off loosely purlwise.

NECKBAND

With 2¼ mm (size 13) needles and C, pick up and k 110 sts around neck, beg at right front neck edge (right side facing).
Work 5 rows in k1 p1 rib.
Frill 1 Change to 3¼ mm (size 10) needles and work 1 row, inc into every st to end, then pick up and k 4 sts down side of ribbing (224 sts). Join on A.
Next row work in k1 p1 rib to end and then pick up and k 4 sts down side of ribbing (228 sts), then k 1 row and cast off loosely purlwise.
Frill 2 Turn Frill 1 down onto right side of work and with 2¼ mm (size 13) needles and C, pick up and k 110 sts on inside of neckband in exactly the same place as Frill 1. Work 7 rows in k1 p1 rib, then change to 3¼ mm (size 10) needles and work 1 row, inc into every st to end, and then pick up and k 6 sts down side of ribbing (226 sts). Join on D.
Next row work in k1 p1 rib to end and then pick up and k 6 sts down side of ribbing (232 sts), then k 1 more row and cast off loosely purlwise.
Frill 3 Turn Frills 1 and 2 down onto right side of work and with 2¼ mm (size 13) needles and C, pick up and k 110 sts on inside of neckband in exactly the same place as Frills 1 and 2. Work 11 rows in k1 p1 rib, then change to 3¼ mm (size 10) needles and work 1 row, inc into every st to end, and then pick up and k 10 sts down side of ribbing (230 sts). Join on E.
Next row work in k1 p1 rib to end and then pick up and k 10 sts down side of ribbing (240 sts), then k 1 more row and cast off loosely purlwise.

BUTTONHOLE BAND

Frill With 2¼ mm (size 13) needles and C, pick up and k 104 sts between top of welt and neck edge (do not include the welt). Work 4 rows in k1 p1 rib, then change to 3¼ mm (size 10) needles and work 1 row, inc into every st, then pick up and k 4 sts down side of ribbing (212 sts). Join on E.
Next row work in k1 p1 rib to end and then pick up and k 4 sts down side of ribbing (216 sts), then k 1 row and cast off loosely purlwise.
Turn Frill down onto right side of work and with 2¼ mm (size 13) needles and C, pick up and k 125 sts in exactly the same place, including Welt and Frills, beg just inside inc row of Frill 1.
Rows 1–3 work in k1 p1 rib, then make buttonholes.
Row 4 rib 2, cast off 6, *rib until there are 17 sts on right-hand needle, cast off 6; rep from * to last 2 sts, rib 2.
Row 5 cont in k1 p1 rib, casting on 6 sts over the 6 buttonholes.
Rows 6–9 work in k1 p1 rib.
Row 10 p (to make foldline).
Rows 11–14 work in k1 p1 rib.
Rows 15 and 16 as rows 4 and 5.
Rows 17–19 work in k1 p1 rib, then cast off loosely in rib. Fold band to inside along foldline and stitch down neatly, neatening around buttonholes with a small buttonhole st.

BUTTONBAND

Frill Work exactly as given for Buttonhole band Frill. Turn Frill down onto right side of work and with 2¼ mm (size 13) needles and C, pick up and k 126 sts in exactly the same place, including Welt and Frills, then work 9 rows in k1 p1 rib. P next row (to make foldline), work 9 more rows in k1 p1 rib, then cast off loosely in rib. Fold band to inside along foldline and stitch down neatly. Sew on buttons.

SLEEVE INSERTION

With 2¼ mm (size 13) circular needle and C, pick up and k 132 sfs around top edge of sleeve. Loop short strand brightly coloured wool round 1st st of round as marker and then p 4 rounds. Leave sts on needle. Place sleeve in armhole with right sides tog, matching underarm panels, and graft (see page 155) tog.
Frill With set of 4 double-pointed 2¼ mm (size 13) needles and C, pick up and k 104 sts around top edge of sleeve, except underarm panel, along round indicated by marker. Work 4 rows in k1 p1 rib, then change to 3¼ mm (size 10) needles and work 1 row, inc into every st, and then pick up and k 4 sts down side of ribbing (212 sts). Join on E.
Next row work in k1 p1 rib to end and then pick up and k 4 sts down side of ribbing (216 sts), then k 1 more row and cast off loosely purlwise.
Rep for 2nd sleeve.

MAGICIAN

Of all my designs, this has been the most fun to create. Who could resist rearranging the heavens and playing with sparkling stars and moons? It uses plied wool, which is thicker than unplied, and is quickly knitted. The sleeves taper at the wrist. The variegated stars and moons leave you free to experiment with the sparkling effect, which can be brightened or subdued according to how you mix the colours. I like using the dark colours on the outside of the motifs, working gradually to a pale centre. Women can wear this roomy jersey as easily as men. Some of the dye recipes can be doubled up, which will save time.

MATERIALS
Circular 2¼ mm (size 13) needle 80 cm (31½ in) long
Set of 4 double-pointed 2¼ mm (size 13) needles
2 circular 4 mm (size 8) needles 40 cm (16 in) and
80 cm (31½ in) long
Pair of 4 mm (size 8) needles
8 stitch holders

Top of garment

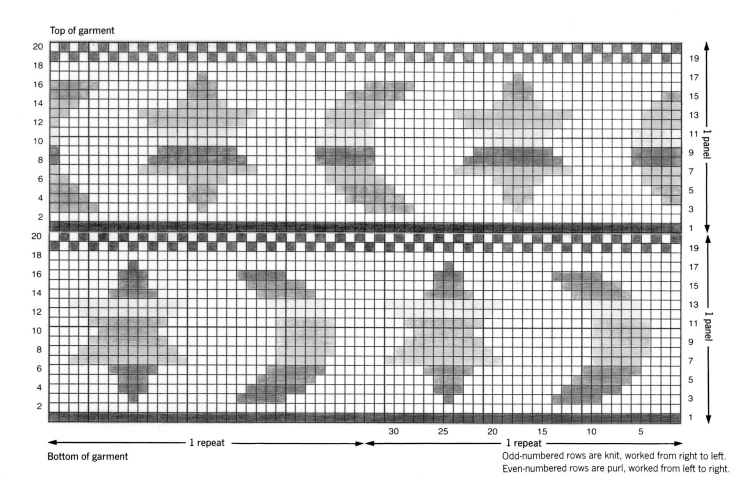

1 panel

1 panel

1 repeat

Bottom of garment

1 repeat

Odd-numbered rows are knit, worked from right to left.
Even-numbered rows are purl, worked from left to right.

WEIGHT OF YARN AND COLOURS
Plied yarn
Navy (A) 345 g (12 oz)
Dark grey (B) 230 g (8 oz)
Grey (C) 230 g (8 oz)
Dark Indigo blue (D) 170 g (6 oz)
Ochre (E1) 85 g (3 oz)
Red (E2) 57 g (2 oz)
Walnut (E3) 85 g (3 oz)
Yellow (E4) 85 g (3 oz)
Natural (E5) 85 g (3 oz)

MEASUREMENTS
Length from top of shoulder to bottom edge of sweater:
76 cm (30 in)
Actual width all round at underarm: 122 cm (48 in)
Sleeve length: 65 cm (26 in)

TENSION
Over pattern, using 4 mm (size 8) needles, 23 stitches
and 24 rows to 10 cm (4 in).

IMPORTANT
● Change colours of wool for star and moon motifs
every 2–3 rows to give a random effect.
● Twist wools at back of work every 1–2 stitches to

avoid making holes, but do not pull tight.
● When working st st using just one colour twist a
spare ball of the same colour yarn across the back of
work to keep the thickness of the garment even.
● The sweater is knitted on a circular needle as far as
the underarm, so every round of the chart up to that
point is knit.
● When using the circular needles, take great care on
the first round to ensure that the stitches are not twisted
around the needle.
● When knitting in the round, loop a short strand of
brightly coloured wool around the first stitch each time
you begin a round so that you can find the beginning.
● The sleeves are knitted on a circular needle and
worked from shoulder to cuff, so remember to reverse
the order of the pattern, that is, work from row 20–1.
● There are 4 background colours so always check
that you are using the correct colour, as follows:

BODY	SLEEVE (top to bottom)
Panel 1: A	Panel 1: A
Panel 2: B	Panel 2: B
Panel 3: C	Panel 3: C
Panel 4: D	Panel 4: D
Panel 5: C	Panel 5: C
Panel 6: B	Panel 6: B
Panel 7: A	Panel 7: A
Panel 8: B	

INSTRUCTIONS
FRONT AND BACK
With 2¼ mm (size 13) circular needle and A, cast on
240 sts. Work 24 rounds in k1 p1 rib.
Inc round *k4, inc into next st; rep from * to end (288
sts).
Change to 4 mm (size 8) 80 cm (31½ in) long circular
needle and work panels 1 and 2 alternately for 100
rounds. (Work panels 1 and 2 alternately throughout
pattern.)

Divide for front and back
Slip 1st 14 sts onto a st holder (Holder 1) for underarm,
then patt 116 sts.
Leave rem sts on circular needle and, with pair of 4 mm
(size 8) needles, work straight on these 116 sts for
back, until 3 complete panels and 1 row have been
worked.
Row 2 (wrong side facing) patt 39 sts, turn.
Row 3 k2 tog, patt to end.
Row 4 patt 38 sts, turn.
Row 5 k2 tog, patt to end (37 sts), then slip these 37
sts onto a st holder for left back shoulder.
With wrong side facing slip next 38 sts onto a st holder
for back neck, then cont on rem 39 sts as follows:
Row 2 (wrong side facing) patt to end.
Row 3 patt to last 2 sts, k2 tog, turn.

Row 4 as chart.

Row 5 patt to last 2 sts, k2 tog, turn (37 sts), then slip sts onto a st holder for right back shoulder.
With right side facing return to rem sts and slip next 28 sts onto a st holder (Holder 2) for underarm. Patt 116 sts and slip rem 14 sts onto Holder 1.
With pair of 4 mm (size 8) needles, work 2 complete panels and 4 rows.

Row 5 patt 43 sts, turn.

Row 6 cast off 2 sts, patt to end.

Row 7 as chart.

Row 8 cast off 2 sts, patt to end.

Row 9 as chart.

Row 10 cast off 1 st, patt to end.

Row 11 as chart.

Row 12 cast off 1 st, patt to end (37 sts).
Work straight until rest of this panel and 6 rows of next have been worked, then slip sts onto a st holder for left front shoulder. Slip next 30 sts onto a st holder for front neck and then work rem 43 sts (right side facing) as follows:

Row 5 cast off 2 sts, patt to end.

Row 6 as chart.

Row 7 cast off 2 sts, patt to end.

Row 8 as chart.

Row 9 cast off 1 st, patt to end.

Row 10 as chart.

Row 11 cast off 1 st, patt to end (37 sts) and then work straight until work matches left side of neck. Leave sts on a spare needle for right front shoulder.

Shoulder seams

Block (see page 155) garment and press carefully on wrong side using a damp cloth. Graft (see page 155) 37 sts for right front shoulder to right back shoulder and left front shoulder to left back shoulder (right sides together). Weave in any loose ends using darning needle (do not just cut them off).

SLEEVES

Remember to k all rounds and panels in rev order – from row 20–1.
With right side facing and 4 mm (size 8) 40 cm (16 in) circular needle and A, slip last 14 sts from Holder 1 onto left needle and k them. Then pick up and k 66 sts up to shoulder seam, 66 sts down to st holder and then k the 14 sts left on Holder (160 sts). Then work from chart, beg at st 32, row 19, until 2 complete panels and rows 20–3 of next panel have been worked.

Row 2 *k3, k2 tog; rep from * to end (128 sts), then work straight until 4 complete panels and rows 20–3 (counting from beg) have been worked.

Row 2 *k2, k2 tog; rep from * to end (96 sts), then work straight until 6 complete panels and rows 20–3 (counting from beg) have been worked. Change to set of 4 double-pointed 2¼ mm (size 13) needles.

Row 2 *k1, k2 tog; rep from * to end (64 sts), then work 24 rounds in A in k1 p1 rib, then cast off loosely in rib. Weave in any loose ends using a darning needle. Press sleeves carefully on wrong side using a damp cloth.

NECKBAND

With right side facing and set of 4 double-pointed 2¼ mm (size 13) needles and A, k the 38 sts for back of neck, pick up and k 27 sts down left side of neck, k the 30 sts for front of neck and pick up and k 27 sts up right side of neck (right side facing; 122 sts). Work 9 rounds in k1 p1 rib. P next round (to make foldline) and work 9 more rounds in k1 p1 rib, then cast off loosely in rib. Fold band to inside along foldline and stitch down neatly.

STARS AND MOONS HAT

MATERIALS

Pair of 5 mm (size 6) needles
Approximately 130 by 7 cm (1 yd 12¾ in by 2¾ in) strip of 115 g (4 oz) polyester wadding
Medium weight card (enough to accommodate 6 circles each 8 cm [3 in] in diameter)

WEIGHT OF YARN AND COLOURS

PLIED YARN   (or 2 strands of ordinary yarn knitted together)
Navy (A)   85 g (3 oz)
Dark Indigo blue (B)   85 g (3 oz)
Yellow (C)   85 g (3 oz)
Grey (D)   14 g (½ oz)
Walnut (E)   14 g (½ oz)

TENSION

Over pattern, using 5 mm (size 6) needles, 18 stitches and 24 rows to 10 cm (4 in).

INSTRUCTIONS

BRIM

With 5 mm (size 6) needles and A, cast on 48 sts and work from chart, beg at st 1, row 1.

Rows 1 and 2 as chart.

Row 3 dec 1 st at beg of row and inc 1 st at end of row.

Row 4 as chart.

Rows 5–86 as chart, dec and inc each alternate row as row 3, then cast off loosely in A. Weave in any loose ends using a darning needle (do not just cut them off) and press carefully on wrong side using a damp cloth. Bring cast on edge and cast off edge tog (right sides tog) and sew neat seam using small back stitches.

CROWN

With 5 mm (size 6) needles and B, cast on 104 sts and work 40 rows in st st, then shape each alternate row as follows (right side facing).

Row 1 k5, *k3 tog, k10*; rep from * to * to last 8 sts, k3 tog, k5 (88 sts).

Row 2 (and each alternate row) p.

Row 3 k4, *k3 tog, k8; rep from * to * last 7 sts, k3 tog, k4 (72 sts).

Row 5 k3, *k3 tog, k6*; rep from * to * to last 6 sts, k3 tog, k3 (56 sts).

Row 7 k2, *k3 tog, k4*; rep from * to * to last 5 sts, k3 tog, k2 (40 sts).

Row 9 k1, *k3 tog, k2*; rep from * to * to last 4 sts. K3 tog, k1 (24 sts).

Row 11 *k3 tog*; rep from * to * to end (8 sts). Keep sts on needle. Cut off wool, leaving a length of about 10 cm (4 in), then, using a darning needle, thread this through sts on needle, pull tightly and fasten off securely. Bring side edges of crown tog (right sides tog) and sew a neat seam using small back stitches.

FINISHING

Place left-hand edge of brim (wrong side facing) along inside cast on edge of crown (wrong side facing), matching brim seam with crown seam, and sew neat seam using small back stitches. Fold strip of wadding in half lengthways and lay it on wrong side of brim below seam. Bring right-hand edge of brim up over wadding and slip stitch it to cast on edge of crown. Then, with tiny, loose slip stitches, stitch brim to crown again about 2 cm (¾ in) up from cast on edge of crown.

Cast off edge

Cast on edge

Pompons

With A, make 3 plaits (23, 31 and 39 cm; 9, 12 and 15½ in long), using 3 strands of yarn for each plait. Leave on one side.

Cut out 6 circles from the card, approximately 8 cm (3 in) in diameter. In the centre of each circle, mark another, approximately 2 cm (¾ in) in diameter and cut them out. Place 2 of the card rings tog and, using one of the colours you used for the moon and star motifs, thread a darning needle and wind it evenly round the card ring, from inner to outer edge, until the inner circle

is tightly filled (make any knots on outer edge of ring). Then insert tip of some sharp scissors between the 2 card rings and cut the wool all round the outer edge. Pull the 2 card rings slightly apart and tie a length of the same colour wool tightly round all the strands of wool in the middle. Attach 1 end of 1 of the plaits securely to this, then tear off the 2 card rings. Snip off any uneven ends around pompon so you have a good smooth shape. Make 2 more pompons in the same way and then attach plaits securely to top of hat by passing them through hole and stitching them to side seam.

POPPIES

Only a small amount of dyeing is required for this cardigan, as the background is natural. The knitting is done sideways, and it is important to weave the wool to the end of each row or the tension goes completely crazy. The poppies are bold and stand out well against the background. It's a cardigan I wear a lot on cool summer evenings.

MATERIALS
Pair of 2¼ mm (size 13) needles
Set of 4 double-pointed 2¼ mm (size 13) needles
Pair of 3¼ mm (size 10) needles
6 buttons

WEIGHT OF YARN AND COLOURS
Natural (A)   340 g (12 oz)
Blue green (B)   170 g (6 oz)
Crimson (C)   115 g (4 oz)
Burgundy (D)   42 g (1½ oz)

MEASUREMENTS
Length from top of shoulder to bottom edge of cardigan: 57 cm (22½ in)
Actual width all round at underarm: 127 cm (50 in)
Sleeve length: 56 cm (22 in)

TENSION
Over pattern, using 3¼ mm (size 10) needles, 28 sts and 30 rows to 10 cm (4 in).

IMPORTANT
● Twist wools at back of work every 1–2 sts to avoid making holes, but do not pull tight.
● When working st st using just one colour twist a spare ball of the same colour yarn across the back of work to keep the thickness of the garment even.
● This garment is knitted sideways, beginning at left front edge, and the sleeves are also knitted sideways.

INSTRUCTIONS
FRONTS AND BACK

Panel 1
With 3¼ mm (size 10) needles and A, cast on 104 sts.

Work 2 rows in st st, then work from chart, beg at st 21, row 19.
Rows 19–26 as chart.
Cont working from chart, inc alternate rows as follows.
Rows 27 and 29 With right side facing inc 1 st at end (neck edge) of row.
Rows 31 and 33 cast on 2 sts at end (neck edge) of row.
Rows 35 and 37 cast on 3 sts at end (neck edge) of row.
Rows 39 and 41 cast on 5 sts at end (neck edge) of row (126 sts).
Row 42 as chart, then work 4 rows rev st st in B as follows:
Row 1 k.
Row 2 k.
Row 3 p.
Row 4 k.

Panel 2
Work from chart, beg at st 21, row 1.
Rows 1–41 as chart, omitting stem beg 4th poppy.
Row 42 With wrong side facing cast off 52 sts (neck edge), patt to end (74 sts), then work 4 rows rev st st in B as before.

Panel 3 (underarm panel)
Work from chart, beg at st 21, row 1.
Rows 1–42 as chart, omitting stem beg 3rd poppy, then work 4 rows rev st st in B as before.

Panel 4
Work from chart, beg at st 21, row 1.
Row 1 Patt to end of row (neck edge), cast on 52 sts (126 sts).
Rows 2–42 as chart, omitting stem beg 4th poppy, then work 4 rows rev st st in B as before.

Panel 5
Work from chart, beg at st 21, row 1.
Rows 1–2 as chart.
Rows 3–11 dec 1 st at end (neck edge) of 1st and every following 4th row (123 sts).
Rows 12–31 as chart.
Rows 32–40 inc 1 st at beg (neck edge) of 32nd and every following 4th row (126 sts), omitting stem beg 4th poppy.
Rows 41–42 as chart.
Work 4 rows rev st st in B as before.

Panel 6
Work from chart, beg at st 21, row 1.
Rows 1–41 as chart, omitting stem beg 4th poppy.
Row 42 With wrong side facing cast off 52 sts (neck

edge), patt to end (74 sts), then work 4 rows rev st st in B as before.

Panel 7 (underarm panel)
Work from chart, beg at st 21, row 1.
Rows 1–42 as chart, omitting stem beg 3rd poppy, then work 4 rows rev st st in B as before.

Panel 8
Work from chart, beg at st 21, row 1.
Row 1 Patt to end of row (neck edge), cast on 52 sts (126 sts).
Rows 2–42 as chart, omitting stem beg 4th poppy, then work 4 rows rev st st in B as before.

Panel 9
Work from chart, beg at st 21, row 1.
Rows 1–3 as chart.
Cont working from chart, dec alternate rows as follows.
Rows 4 and 6 cast off 5 sts (neck edge), patt to end.
Rows 8 and 10 cast off 3 sts (neck edge), patt to end.
Rows 12 and 14 cast off 2 sts (neck edge), patt to end.
Rows 16 and 18 cast off 1 st (neck edge), patt to end (104 sts).
Rows 19–24 as chart. Work 2 rows st st with A, then cast off loosely.
Weave in any loose ends using a darning needle (do not just cut them off). Block (see page 155) garment and press carefully on wrong side using a damp cloth.

Shoulder seams
With right side facing and 2¼ mm (size 13) needles and B, pick up and k 40 sts along right front shoulder. K 1 row, p 1 row and k 1 row. Leave sts on a spare needle. With right side facing and 2¼ mm (size 13) needles and B, pick up and k 40 sts along right back shoulder. Leave sts on needle, then graft (see page 155) right front shoulder to right back shoulder (right sides together). Rep for left shoulder.

SLEEVES
With 3¼ mm (size 10) needles and A, cast on 133 sts. Work 4 complete panels from chart, beg at st 23, row 1 and omitting stem beg 4th poppy, with 4 rows rev st st in B between each panel and end with 4 rows rev st st. Leave sts on needle, then weave in any loose ends using a darning needle (do not just cut them off). Press carefully on wrong side using a damp cloth. Graft (see page 155) sts on needle to cast on edge (right sides together).

Cuffs
With right side facing and set of 4 double-pointed 2¼ mm (size 13) needles and A, pick up and k 122 sts along lower edge of sleeve, ensuring patt is correct.
Round 1 *k2 tog; rep from * to end (61 sts).
Round 2 k to last 2 sts, k2 tog (60 sts), then work 43 more rounds in k1 p1 rib. Join on B, work 2 rounds in k1 p1 rib. Join on 2nd strand B, cast off loosely in rib.

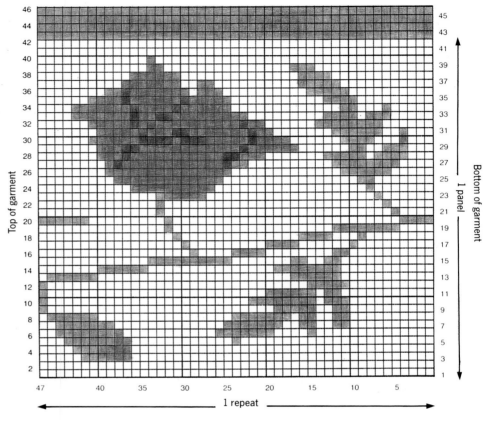

Odd-numbered rows are knit, worked from right to left.
Even-numbered rows are purl, worked from left to right.

WELT
With right side facing and 2¼ mm (size 13) needles and A, pick up and k 260 sts along lower edge of fronts and back. Work 43 rows in k1 p1 rib, join on B and work 2 rows in k1 p1 rib, then join on 2nd strand B and cast off loosely in rib.

NECKBAND
With right side facing and 2¼ mm (size 13) needles and A, pick up and k 110 sts around neck. Work 7 rows in k1 p1 rib, then join on B and work 2 rows in k1 p1 rib. P 1 row (to make foldline) then work 2 rows in k1 p1 rib. Join on A and work 7 more rows in k1 p1 rib, then cast off loosely in rib. Fold band to inside along foldline and stitch down neatly.

BUTTONHOLE BAND
With right side facing and 2¼ mm (size 13) needles and A, pick up and k 147 sts up right front edge.
Rows 1–4 work in k1 p1 rib, then make buttonholes.
Row 5 rib 3, cast off 6, *rib 21 (including st on needle), cast off 6; rep from * to last 3 sts, rib 3.
Row 6 cont in k1 p1 rib, casting on 6 sts over the 6 buttonholes.
Row 7 work in k1 p1 rib.
Rows 8–9 join on B and work in k1 p1 rib.

Row 10 p (to make foldline).
Rows 11–12 work in k1 p1 rib. Break off B.
Row 13 join on A and work in k1 p1 rib.
Rows 14–15 as rows 5 and 6.
Rows 16–19 work in k1 p1 rib, then cast off loosely in rib. Fold band to inside along foldline and stitch down neatly, using small buttonhole stitch around buttonholes.

BUTTONBAND
With right side facing and 2¼ mm (size 13) needles and A, pick up and k 147 sts down left front edge. Work 7 rows in k1 p1 rib in A, join on B and work 2 more rows in k1 p1 rib. P 1 row (to make foldline) then work 2 more rows in k1 p1 rib. Break off B. Join on A and work 7 more rows in k1 p1 rib, then cast off loosely in rib. Fold band to inside along foldline and stitch down neatly. Sew on buttons.

SLEEVE INSERTION
With set of 4 double-pointed 2¼ mm (size 13) needles and B, pick up and k 132 sts around top edge of sleeve (right side facing). Work 3 rounds in p, then cast off loosely knitwise. Rep for 2nd sleeve. Place sleeves in armholes with right sides tog, matching underarm panels. Sew seams using small back sts. Weave in loose ends using a darning needle (do not just cut them off).

ADULT TULIP

I have a soft spot for the Tulip jacket. It was my first success at creating a design to be used exclusively with natural dyes, one that would show off the range of the colours, and their brightness. The rounded patterning and generous shapes give the tulips a life of their own. It's an enjoyable jacket for a new knitter to tackle: the knitting has a rhythm, and there's freedom to play with the shades of red and pink within the tulips. The blues, greys and greens are all soft vibrant colours, and the theatrical sleeves add to its impact.

MATERIALS
Pair of 2¼ mm (size 13) needles
Set of 4 double-pointed 2¼ mm (size 13) needles
2 pairs of 3¼ mm (size 10) needles
Circular 3¼ mm (size 10) needle 40 cm (16 in) long
9 stitch holders
9 buttons

WEIGHT OF YARN AND COLOURS
Green (A)   115 g (4 oz)
Scarlet (B1)   57 g (2 oz)
Crimson (B2)   57 g (2 oz)
Red (B3)   57 g (2 oz)
Dark Indigo blue (C)   280 g (10 oz)
Dark grey (D)   230 g (8 oz)
Medium Indigo blue (E)   170 g (6 oz)
Grey (F)   115 g (4 oz)

MEASUREMENTS
Length from top of shoulder to bottom edge of jacket:
76 cm (30 in)
Actual width all round at underarm: 129.5 cm (51 in)
Sleeve length: 56 cm (22 in)

TENSION

Over pattern, using 3¼ mm (size 10) needles, 28 stitches and 32 rows to 10 cm (4 in).

IMPORTANT

• Change shade of red for tulip motif every 2–3 rows to give a random effect.
• Twist wools at back of work every 1–2 sts to avoid making holes, but do not pull tight.
• When working st st using just one colour twist a spare ball of the same colour yarn across the back of work to keep the thickness of the garment even.
• To make ridge on right side of work between each panel, rows 1 and 2 of the chart are knit.
• When using the circular needle for the sleeves, remember that all rounds of chart are knit (except round 1, which is purl) and must be worked in reverse order as you are knitting from shoulder to cuff, that is, you work from row 24 to 1.
• When using the circular needle, loop a short strand of brightly coloured wool around the first stitch each time you begin a round so that you can find the beginning easily.

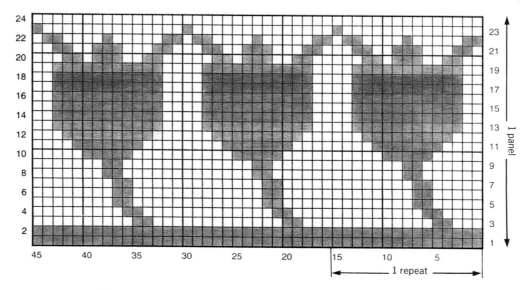

Odd-numbered rows are knit, worked from right to left.
Even-numbered rows are purl, worked from left to right.

INSTRUCTIONS
FRONTS AND BACK

With 2¼ mm (size 13) needles and 2 strands A, cast on 310 sts. Cont with single strand and work 2 rows in k1 p1 rib. Join on B1 and work 2 more rows in k1 p1 rib. Join on C and work 41 more rows in k1 p1 rib.
Inc row rib 20, *inc into next st, rib 4; rep from * to last 20 sts, rib 20 (364 sts). Then join on A, change to 3¼ mm (size 10) needles and work from chart, beg at st 1, row 1, keeping 1st 2 and last 2 sts plain as these are the front edges. Work 2 complete panels, ending 2nd panel with row 24 and working panel 1 in background colour D and panel 2 in background colour E.

Pocket linings

Lay work on one side. With 3¼ mm (size 10) needles and background colour D, cast on 42 sts. For Pocket lining 1, beg at st 28, row 1 of chart, for Pocket lining 2, beg at st 22, row 1 and work 2 panels as chart. Leave each Pocket lining on one of 2nd pair of 3¼ mm (size 10) needles. Return to main body of work.
Patt 29 sts, slip next 42 sts onto a st holder, then join in Pocket lining 1, k from its needle, and patt to last 71 sts. Slip next 42 sts onto a st holder, then join in Pocket lining 2, k from its needle, and work to end. Work straight, working panel 3 in background colour F, panel 4 in background colour C and then rep background colours in same order, until 6 panels, ending panel 6 with row 24, have been worked.

Divide for fronts and back

With right side facing, patt 70 sts, turn. Cont in patt on these 70 sts until 8 panels and 6 rows of panel 9 (counting from beg) have been worked.
Row 7 With right side facing, cast off 16 sts, patt to end (54 sts).
Row 8 patt to last 3 sts, p2 tog, p1.
Row 9 k1, k2 tog, patt to end.
Rep last 2 rows until 44 sts rem.
Work straight until 9th panel has been worked, then k 2 rows with A. Slip these 44 sts onto a st holder, for right front shoulder grafting.
With right side facing return to rem sts, slip next 42 sts onto a st holder for right underarm and then patt next 140 sts for back and turn. Work straight on these 140 sts until 8 panels and 16 rows (from beg) have been worked.
Row 17 patt 47 sts, k2 tog, k1, turn.
Row 18 p1, p2 tog, patt to end.
Row 19 patt to last 3 sts, k2 tog, k1 (47 sts).
Rep last 2 rows until 44 sts rem, then work straight until 9th panel has been worked. K 1 row with A and slip sts onto a st holder for right back shoulder grafting.
Slip next 40 sts for back neck onto a st holder and work rem 50 sts as follows:
Row 17 k1 k2 tog, patt to end.
Row 18 patt to last 3 sts, p2 tog, p1.
Row 19 k1, k2 tog, patt to end.
Rep last 2 rows until 44 sts rem, then work straight until 9th panel has been worked. K 1 row with A, and slip sts onto a st holder for left back shoulder grafting.
With right side facing slip next 42 sts onto a st holder for left underarm and then patt rem 70 sts. Work straight

until 8 panels and 5 rows have been worked from beg.
Row 6 cast off 16 sts, patt to end (54 sts).
Row 7 patt to last 3 sts, k2 tog, k1.
Row 8 p1, p2 tog, patt to end.
Rep last 2 rows until 44 sts rem, then work straight until 9th panel has been worked. K2 rows with A, then slip sts onto a st holder for left front shoulder grafting.

Pocket tops

With right side facing and 2¼ mm (size 13) needles and A, slip the 42 sts for pocket from st holder onto needles and work as follows:
Rows 1 and 2 k.
Rows 3–5 join on C and work in k1 p1 rib.
Rows 6 and 7 join on B1 and work in k1 p1 rib.
Rows 8 and 9 join on A and work in k1 p1 rib, then join on 2nd strand A and cast off loosely in rib.
Stitch down neatly and sew Pocket lining into place using a small slip st. Rep for 2nd pocket.

Shoulder seams

Block (see page 155) garment and press carefully on wrong side using a damp cloth, but do not press ribbing. Graft (see page 155) right front shoulder to right back shoulder (right sides together). Rep for left shoulder. Weave in any loose ends using a darning needle (do not just cut them off).

SLEEVES

Remember to k all rounds (except round 1 which is p) and work chart in rev order – from row 24–1.
With right side facing and 3¼ mm (size 10) circular needle and A, slip last 21 sts for underarm from st

holder onto needle and k them. Then pick up and k 138 sts around armhole and k rem 21 sts on holder (180 sts). P 1 round with A. Work 6 complete panels, with background colours in the order E, D, C, F, E and D, ending with round 3. Change to set of 4 double-pointed 2¼ mm (size 13) needles and join on A.

Dec round 1 *k3, k2 tog; rep from * to end (144 sts).
Dec round 2 *p2, p2 tog; rep from * to end (108 sts). Change to C.
Dec round 3 *k1, k2 tog; rep from * to end (72 sts).
Dec round 4 *k4, k2 tog*; rep from * to * to end (60 sts).
Work 41 rounds in k1 p1 rib in C. Join on B1 and work 2 more rounds in k1 p1 rib, then join on A and work 2 more rounds in rib. Join on 2nd strand A and cast off loosely in rib. Weave in any loose ends using a darning needle (do not just cut them off). Press carefully on wrong side using a damp cloth, but do not press ribbing.

NECKBAND

With right side facing and 2¼ mm (size 13) needles and C, pick up and k 35 sts between right front neck edge and st holder at back of neck. Slip the 40 sts from holder onto needle and k them, then pick up and k 35 sts down to left front neck edge (110 sts). Work 5 rows in k1 p1 rib, then join on B1 and work 2 rows in rib, then join on A and work 2 rows in rib. P next row (to make foldline), then work 2 rows in rib, then join on B1 and work 2 rows in rib, then join on C and work 5 rows in rib, then cast off loosely in rib. Fold band to inside along foldline and stitch down neatly.

BUTTONHOLE BAND

With right side facing and 2¼ mm (size 13) needles and C, pick up and k 250 sts up right front.
Rows 1–3 work in k1 p1 rib, then make buttonholes.
Row 4 rib 2, cast off 6 sts, *rib 24 (including st left on needle), cast off 6; rep from * to last 2 sts, rib 2.
Row 5 cont in k1 p1 rib, casting on 6 sts over the 9 buttonholes.
Rows 6 and 7 join on B1 and work in k1 p1 rib.
Rows 8 and 9 join on A and work in k1 p1 rib.
Row 10 p (to make foldline).
Rows 11 and 12 cont in A k1 p1 rib.
Rows 13 and 14 join on B1 and work in k1 p1 rib.
Rows 15 and 16 join on C and work as rows 4 and 5.
Rows 17–19 work in k1 p1 rib, then cast off loosely in rib. Fold band to inside along foldline and stitch down neatly, using small buttonhole st around buttonholes.

BUTTONBAND

With right side facing and 2¼ mm (size 13) needles and C, pick up and k 250 sts down left front. Work 5 rows in k1 p1 rib, then join on B1 and work 2 rows in rib, then join on A and work 2 rows in rib. P next row (to make foldline), then work 2 rows in rib, then join on B1 and work 2 rows in rib, then join on C and work 5 rows in rib, then cast off loosely in rib. Fold band to inside along foldline and stitch down neatly. Sew on buttons.

CHILD'S TULIP

Of all the flowers used in decoration, the simple shape of the tulip is the most dominant. Tulips embellish European and North American folk art, and stylized versions can be found on furniture, textiles and ceramics. Its stately silhouette is so obviously floral, and its leaves and stem are easily worked into the pattern. This design evolved out of my first attempt at playing with noughts and crosses on graph paper, and its rounded, flowing shape counters the effect of the horizontal lines of the pattern.

MATERIALS

Pair of 2¼ mm (size 13) needles
Set of 4 double-pointed 2¼ mm (size 13) needles
Pair of 3¼ mm (size 10) needles
Circular 3¼ mm (size 10) needle 40 cm (16 in) long
6 stitch holders
6 buttons

WEIGHT OF YARN AND COLOURS

Blue green (A) 115 g (4 oz)
Scarlet (B1) 28 g (1 oz)
Crimson (B2) 28 g (1 oz)
Red (B3) 28 g (1 oz)
Magenta (B4) 28 g (1 oz)
Dark Indigo blue (C) 115 g (4 oz)
Grey (D) 115 g (4 oz)
Pale Indigo blue (E) 57 g (2 oz)

MEASUREMENTS

Length from top of shoulder to bottom edge of jacket: 38 cm (15 in)
Actual width all round at underarm: 86 cm (34 in)
Sleeve length: 35.5 cm (14 in)

TENSION

Over pattern, using 3¼ mm (size 10) needles, 32 stitches and 32 rows to 10 cm (4 in).

IMPORTANT

● Change shade of red for tulip motif every 2–3 rows to give a random effect.
● Twist wools at back of work every 1–2 stitches to avoid making holes, but do not pull tight.
● When working st st using just one colour twist a spare ball of the same colour yarn across the back of work to keep the thickness of the garment even.
● To make ridge on right side of work between each panel, rows 1 and 2 of the chart are knit.
● When using the circular needle for the sleeves, remember that all rounds of chart are knit (except round 1, which is purl) and must be worked in reverse order as you are knitting from shoulder to cuff, that is, you work from row 24 to 1.
● When using the circular needle, loop a short strand of brightly coloured wool around the first stitch each time you begin a round so that you can find the beginning easily.

INSTRUCTIONS
FRONTS AND BACK

With 2¼ mm (size 13) needles and A, cast on 240 sts and work 2 rows in k1 p1 rib. Join on B1 and work 2 more rows in k1 p1 rib.
Join on C and work 29 more rows in k1 p1 rib.
Inc row *rib 7, inc into next st; rep from * to end (270 sts).
Then join on A, change to 3¼ mm (size 10) needles and work from chart, beg at st 1, row 1. Work 2 complete panels, ending 2nd panel with row 24, working panel 1 in background colour D, panel 2 in background colour E and tulips in B shades in random numbers of rows.

Divide for fronts and back

With right side facing patt 55 sts, turn. Cont in patt on these 55 sts until 3 panels and 10 rows have been worked (from beg), using background colour C for panel 3 and background colour D for panel 4.
Row 11 With right side facing, cast off 8 sts, patt to end (47 sts).
Rows 12–19 dec 1 st at neck edge on every row (39 sts).
Rows 20–24 as chart. K2 rows with A, then slip sts onto a st holder, for right front shoulder grafting.
With right side facing return to rem 215 sts, slip next 24 sts onto a st holder for right underarm, then patt next 112 sts for back and turn. Work straight on these 112 sts until 3 panels and 16 rows have been worked, working 3rd panel in C and 4th in D.
Row 17 With right side facing patt 46 sts, turn.
Rows 18–24 dec 1 st at neck edge on every row (39 sts). K 1 row with A then slip sts onto a st holder for right back shoulder grafting.
Slip next 20 sts onto a st holder for back neck and work rem 46 sts as follows:
Row 17 patt to end.
Rows 18–24 dec 1 st at neck edge on every row (39 sts). K 1 row with A then slip sts onto a st holder for left back shoulder grafting.

With right side facing slip next 24 sts onto a st holder for left underarm, then patt rem 55 sts. Cont in patt in C and complete panel, then work rows 1–11 of next panel in D.

Row 12 With wrong side facing cast off 8 sts, patt to end (47 sts).

Rows 13–20 dec 1 st at neck edge every row (39 sts).

Rows 21–24 as chart. K 2 rows with A. Leave sts on needle for left front shoulder grafting.

Shoulder seams

Block (see page 155) garment and press carefully on wrong side using a damp cloth. Graft (see page 155) right front shoulder to right back shoulder (right sides together). Rep for left shoulder. Weave in any loose ends using a darning needle (do not just cut them off).

SLEEVES

Remember to k all rounds (except round 1, which is p) and work chart in rev order – from row 24–1.

Slip last 12 sts from st holder for underarm onto 3¼ mm (size 10) circular needle, join on D and k them. Then pick up and k 48 sts up side of armhole between st holder and top of shoulder, pick up and k 48 sts down side of armhole to st holder and k rem 12 sts on holder (120 sts). Work 4 complete panels with background colours in the order D, C, E and D, ending with round 5. Change to set of 4 double-pointed 2¼ mm (size 13) needles.

Round 4 *k1, k2 tog; rep from * to end (80 sts).

Round 3 *k2, k2 tog; rep from * to end (60 sts).

Round 2 k with A.

Round 1 p with A.

Work 30 rounds in k1 p1 rib in C. Join on B1 and work 2 more rounds in k1 p1 rib, then join on A and work 2 more rounds in k1 p1 rib. Join on 2nd strand A and cast off loosely in rib. Weave in any loose ends using a darning needle (do not just cut them off). Press carefully on wrong side using a damp cloth, but do not press ribbing.

NECKBAND

With right side facing and 2¼ mm (size 13) needles and C, pick up and k 37 sts between front neck edge and st holder at back of neck. Slip the 20 sts from st holder onto needle and k them, then pick up and k 37 sts down to left front neck edge (94 sts). Work 5 rows in k1 p1 rib, then join on B1 and work 2 rows in rib, then join on A and work 2 rows in rib. P next row (to make foldline), then work 2 rows in rib, then join on B1 and work 2 rows in rib, then join on C and work 5 rows in rib, then cast off loosely in rib. Fold band to inside along foldline and stitch down neatly.

BUTTONHOLE BAND

With right side facing and 2¼ mm (size 13) needles and C, pick up and k 131 sts up right front edge.

Rows 1–3 work in k1 p1 rib, then make buttonholes.

Row 4 rib 3, cast off 5 sts, *rib 19 (including st on needle), cast off 5 sts; rep from * to last 3 sts, rib 3.

Row 5 cont in k1 p1 rib, casting on 5 sts over the 6 buttonholes.

Rows 6 and 7 join on B1 and work in k1 p1 rib.

Rows 8 and 9 join on A and work in k1 p1 rib.

Row 10 p (to make foldline).

Rows 11 and 12 cont in A in k1 p1 rib.

Rows 13 and 14 join on B1 and work in k1 p1 rib.

Rows 15 and 16 join on C and work as rows 4 and 5.

Rows 17–19 work in k1 p1 rib, then cast off loosely in rib. Fold band to inside along foldline and stitch down neatly, neatening around buttonholes using a small buttonhole st.

BUTTONBAND

With right side facing and 2¼ mm (size 13) needles and C, pick up and k 131 sts down left front. Work 5 rows in k1 p1 rib, then join on B1 and work 2 rows in rib, then join on A and work 2 rows in rib. P next row (to make foldline), then work 2 rows in rib, then join on B1 and work 2 rows in rib, then join on C and work 5 rows in rib, then cast off loosely in rib. Fold band to inside along foldline and stitch down neatly. Sew on buttons.

RAMBLING ROSES

Over the years we have planted about 100 old-fashioned shrub roses in the garden. Their flowering time may be short, but their delicate colouring and delicious scent more than compensate for this. The first pattern, with its blue-and-white background and pink roses, is as subtle as the flowers themselves, and I find the soft colours irresistible. The cardigan is designed to suit infinite colourways, and the second combination is much stronger, with its festive red, green and navy. The ruffles have none of the fussiness of frills. Both patterns are very flattering and feminine, and I have seen both 15- and 80-year-olds looking gorgeous in them.

MATERIALS

Pair of 2¼ mm (size 13) needles
Set of 4 double-pointed 2¼ mm (size 13) needles
Pair of 3¼ mm (size 10) needles
Set of 4 double-pointed 3¼ mm (size 10) needles
Circular 3¼ mm (size 10) needle 80 cm (31½ in) long
6 buttons

WEIGHT OF YARN AND COLOURS

Medium Indigo blue (A) 340 g (12 oz)
Natural (B) 170 g (6 oz)
Blue green (C) 85 g (3 oz)
Pale pink (D1) 85 g (3 oz)
Pink (D2) 85 g (3 oz)

MEASUREMENTS

Length from top of shoulder to bottom edge of cardigan: 53.5 cm (21 in)
Actual width all round at underarm: 117 cm (46 in)
Sleeve length: 57 cm (22½ in)

TENSION

Over pattern, using 3¼ mm (size 10) needles, 30 stitches and 32 rows to 10 cm (4 in).

IMPORTANT

- This garment is knitted sideways, beginning at left front edge, and the sleeves are also knitted sideways.
- There are two background colours so check that you are using the correct colour before beginning each panel: panels 1, 3, 5, 7 and 9 are worked in A and panels 2, 4, 6 and 8 are worked in B.
- Change colours of roses every panel, working pale pink roses on A panels and pink roses on B panels.
- Twist wools at back of work every 1–2 stitches to avoid making holes, but do not pull tight.
- When working st st using just one colour twist a spare ball of the same colour yarn across the back of work to keep the thickness of the garment even.

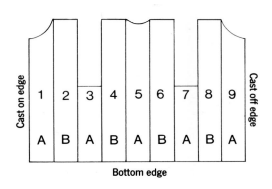

Odd-numbered rows are knit, worked from right to left.
Even-numbered rows are purl, worked from left to right.

INSTRUCTIONS
FRONTS AND BACK
Panel 1

With 3¼ mm (size 10) needles and A, cast on 104 sts. K 1 row, p 1 row then work next 6 rows as chart, beg at st 1, row 21. Cont working from chart and, beginning with a right side row, shape alternate rows for neck as follows:

Rows 27 and 29 inc 1 st at end (neck edge) of row.
Rows 31 and 33 cast on 2 sts at end (neck edge) of row.
Rows 35 and 37 cast on 3 sts at end (neck edge) of row.
Rows 39 and 41 cast on 5 sts at end (neck edge) of row.
Row 42 as chart (126 sts), then work 4 rows rev st st in A as follows:
Row 1 k.
Row 2 k.
Row 3 p.
Row 4 k.

Panel 2

Join on B.
Rows 1–41 as chart.
Row 42 With wrong side facing cast off 52 sts (neck edge), patt to end, then join on A and work 4 rows rev st st as before.

Panel 3 (underarm panel)

Cont in A.
Rows 1–42 as chart, then work 4 rows rev st st as before.

Panel 4

Join on B.
Row 1 patt to end of row (neck edge) and cast on 52 sts.
Rows 2–42 as chart, then join on A and work 4 rows rev st st as before.

Panel 5

Cont in A.
Rows 1–13 dec 1 st at end (neck edge) of 1st and every following 4th row (122 sts).
Rows 14–29 as chart.
Rows 30–42 inc 1 st at beg (neck edge) of 30th and every following 4th row (126 sts), then work 4 rows rev st st as before.

Panel 6

Join on B.
Rows 1–41 as chart.
Row 42 cast off 52 sts (neck edge), patt to end (74 sts), then join on A and work 4 rows rev st st as before.

Panel 7 (underarm panel)

Cont in A.
Rows 1–42 as chart, then work 4 rows rev st st as before.

Panel 8

Join on B.
Row 1 Patt to end of row (neck edge) and cast on 52 sts.
Rows 2–42 as chart, then join on A and work 4 rows rev st st as before.

Panel 9

Cont in A.
Row 1 as chart, then cont working from chart, dec alternate rows as follows:
Rows 2 and 4 cast off 5 sts (neck edge), then patt to end.
Rows 6 and 8 cast off 3 sts (neck edge), then patt to end.
Rows 10 and 12 cast off 2 sts (neck edge), then patt to end.
Rows 14 and 16 cast off 1 st (neck edge), then patt to end.
Rows 17–22 as chart (104 sts). With A, k 1 row, p 1 row then cast off loosely. Weave in any loose ends using

Next round p, then cast off loosely knitwise.

Frill 2 With set of 4 double-pointed 2¼ mm (size 13) needles and A, pick up and k 50 sts along round indicated by marker on inside of cuff. Work 3 rounds in k1 p1 rib, then loop short strand brightly coloured wool round 1st st. Work 2 more rounds in k1 p1 rib, then change to set of 4 double-pointed 3¼ mm (size 10) needles and work 1 round, inc into every st (100 sts). Join on D.

Next round work in k1 p1 rib.

Next round p, then cast off loosely knitwise.

Frill 3 With set of 4 double-pointed 2¼ mm (size 13) needles and A, pick up and k 50 sts around line indicated by 2nd marker on inside of cuff. Work 5 rounds in k1 p1 rib, then change to set of 4 double-pointed 3¼ mm (size 10) needles and work 1 round, inc into every st (100 sts).

Next round k1 p1 to end.

Next round p, then cast off loosely knitwise.

WELT

With right side facing and 2¼ mm (size 13) needles and A, pick up and k 230 sts along lower edge of fronts and back. Work 25 rows in k1 p1 rib. Loop short strand brightly coloured wool round 1st and last st as markers. Work 2 more rows in k1 p1 rib.

Frill 1 Change to 3¼ mm (size 10) needles and work 1 row, inc into every st (460 sts). (Tip: slip sts onto 3¼ mm (size 10) circular needle as this will accommodate all the sts more comfortably and just k from it lengthwise.) Join on C.

Next row work in k1 p1 rib.

Next row k, then cast off loosely purlwise.

Frill 2 With 2¼ mm (size 13) needles and A, pick up and k 230 sts along row indicated by markers on inside of welt and work 3 rows in k1 p1 rib. Loop short strand brightly coloured wool round 1st and last st as markers. Work 2 more rows in k1 p1 rib. Change to 3¼ mm (size 10) needles (or circular needle as before) and work 1 row, inc into every st (460 sts). Join on D.

Next row work in k1 p1 rib.

Next row k, then cast off loosely purlwise.

Frill 3 With 2¼ mm (size 13) needles and A, pick up and k 230 sts along row indicated by 2nd markers on inside of welt. Work 5 rows in k1 p1 rib, then change to 3¼ mm (size 10) needles (or circular needle as before) and work 1 row, inc into every st (460 sts).

Next row work in k1 p1 rib.

Next row k, then cast off loosely purlwise.

NECKBAND

With right side facing and 2¼ mm (size 13) needles and A, pick up and k 110 sts round neck. Work 5 rows in k1 p1 rib.

Frill 1 Change to 3¼ mm (size 10) needles and work 1 row, inc into every st to end, and then pick up and k 4 sts down side of ribbing (224 sts). Join on C.

Next row work in k1 p1 rib to end and then pick up and k 4 more sts down side of ribbing (228 sts), then k 2 more

a darning needle (do not just cut them off). Block (see page 155) garment and press carefully on wrong side using a damp cloth.

SHOULDER SEAMS

With right side facing and 2¼ mm (size 13) needles and A, pick up and k 40 sts along right front shoulder. K 1 row, p 1 row and k 1 row. Leave sts on spare needle. With 2¼ mm (size 13) needles and A, pick up and k 40 sts along right back shoulder and leave sts on needle. Graft (see page 155) right front shoulder to right back shoulder (right sides together). Rep for left shoulder.

SLEEVES

With 3¼ mm (size 10) needles and A, cast on 133 sts. Work 4 complete panels from chart in order A, B, A, B, with 4 rows rev st st in A between each panel and end with 4 rows rev st st in A. Leave sts on needle, then press carefully on wrong side using a damp cloth. Graft

(see page 155) sts on needle to sts of cast on edge (right sides together). Weave in any loose ends using a darning needle (do not just cut them off). Rep for 2nd sleeve.

Cuffs

With set of 4 double-pointed 2¼ mm (size 13) needles and A, pick up and k 122 sts along lower edge of sleeve (right side facing, ensuring patt is right way up, that is, with roses growing up towards shoulder).

Dec round 1 *k2 tog; rep from * to end (61 sts).

Dec round 2 *k4, k2 tog; rep from * to last 7 sts, k4, k3 tog (50 sts), then work 24 more rounds in k1 p1 rib. Loop short strand of brightly coloured wool round 1st st as marker and then work 2 more rounds in k1 p1 rib.

Frill 1 Change to set of 4 double-pointed 3¼ mm (size 10) needles and work 1 round, inc into every st (100 sts), then join on C.

Next round work in k1 p1 rib.

rows and cast off loosely purlwise.

Frill 2 Turn Frill 1 down onto right side of work and with 2¼ mm (size 13) needles and A, pick up and k 110 sts on inside of neckband in exactly the same place as for Frill 1. Work 7 rows in k1 p1 rib, then change to 3¼ mm (size 10) needles and work 1 row, inc into every st to end, and then pick up and k 6 sts down side of ribbing (226 sts). Join on D.

Next row work in k1 p1 rib to end and pick up and k 6 sts down side of ribbing (232 sts), then k 2 more rows and cast off loosely purlwise.

Frill 3 Turn Frills 1 and 2 down onto right side of work and with 2¼ mm (size 13) needles and A, pick up and k 110 sts on inside of neckband in exactly the same place as for Frills 1 and 2. Work 11 rows in k1 p1 rib, then change to 3¼ mm (size 10) needles and work 1 row, inc into every st to end, and then pick up and k 10 sts down side of ribbing (230 sts).

Next row work in k1 p1 rib to end and pick up and k 10 sts down side of ribbing (240 sts), then k 2 more rows and cast off loosely purlwise.

BUTTONHOLE BAND

With right side facing and 2¼ mm (size 13) needles and A, pick up and k 127 sts up right front edge.

Rows 1–3 work in k1 p1 rib, then make buttonholes.

Row 4 rib 3, cast off 6, *rib 17 (including st on needle), cast off 6; rep from * to last 3 sts, rib 3.

Row 5 cont in k1 p1 rib, casting on 6 sts over the 6 buttonholes.

Rows 6–9 work in k1 p1 rib.

Row 10 p (to make foldline).

Rows 11–14 work in k1 p1 rib.

Rows 15 and 16 as rows 4 and 5.

Rows 17–19 work in k1 p1 rib, then cast off loosely in rib. Fold band to inside along foldline and stitch down neatly, neatening around buttonholes using a small buttonhole st.

BUTTONBAND

With right side facing and 2¼ mm (size 13) needles and A, pick up and k 127 sts down left front edge. Work 9 rows in k1 p1 rib, p next row (to make foldline), work 9 more rows in k1 p1 rib, then cast off loosely in rib. Fold band to inside along foldline and stitch down neatly. Sew on buttons.

SLEEVE INSERTION

With right side facing and set of 4 double-pointed 2¼ mm (size 13) needles and A, pick up and k 132 sts around top edge of sleeve. Work 3 rounds in p, then cast off loosely purlwise. Rep for 2nd sleeve. Place sleeves in armholes with right sides tog, matching underarm panels. Sew neat seams using small back sts.

FINISHING

Weave in any loose ends using a darning needle. Press carefully on wrong side using a damp cloth, but do not press ribbing or frills.

FLORAL BAND

MATERIALS

Short circular 4½ mm (size 7) needle
3 mm (size 11) crochet hook
Approximately 60 by 6 cm (2 ft by 2½ in) strip of 115 g (4oz) polyester wadding

WEIGHT OF YARN AND COLOURS

PLIED YARN   (or 2 strands of ordinary yarn knitted together)
Navy (A)   85 g (3 oz)
UNPLIED YARN   (for flowers)
14 g (½ oz) each of 5 colours **(B)**

TENSION

Over stocking stitch, using circular 4½ mm (size 7) needle, 25 stitches and 24 rows to 10 cm (4 in).

IMPORTANT

● The band is knitted on a circular needle so every round is knit.

INSTRUCTIONS

BAND

With 4½ mm (size 7) circular needle and A, cast on 100 sts. Work 40 rounds in st st, then cast off loosely. Weave in any loose ends using a darning needle (do not just cut them off), then press on wrong side using a damp cloth.

FINISHING

Band

Lay band (wrong side up) on a flat surface and lay the strip of wadding down the centre. Bring each side of Band up over wadding to meet along centre and oversew edges neatly in A.

Flower

(See page 157 for Crochet instructions.)
*With 3 mm (size 11) crochet hook and B, work 9 ch and join into a circle by working a sl st through 1st ch.
Round 1 work 6 ch, *1 treble into circle, 3 ch; rep from * 4 times more, then join into a circle by working a sl st through 3rd of 1st 6 ch (forming 6 loops).
Round 2 *work 1 double crochet, 1 half-treble, 3 trebles, 1 half-treble, 1 double crochet into 1st loop; rep from * for rem 5 loops, then join into a circle by working a sl st through 1 st double crochet and cut off wool.
Round 3 rejoin wool at back of work, looping it into top of treble of round 1, *work 5 ch, 1 double crochet in top of next treble of round 1; rep from * 4 more times, work 5 ch, then join to 1st sl st to complete round 1.
Round 4 *work 1 double crochet, 1 half-treble, 5 trebles, 1 half-treble. 1 double crochet into 1st loop; rep from * for rem 5 loops. Fasten off. Weave in any loose ends using a darning needle (do not just cut them off). Rep from *, making 2 flowers in each colour wool. Stitch to band at junctions of petals using matching colour and leaving equal spaces between them.

RIBBONS AND BOWS

This is a simple if large piece of knitting, and the dyeing of the base colours is straightforward. The navy can be dyed in one go by multiplying the recipe by five. Dye the indigo in one batch too so that it all matches. Shade the bows with the four reds in as many different combinations as you like, and the bows will take on a three-dimensional life of their own. I have to confess that this design was originally an error. It turned out longer than intended, so I reworked it to transform it into a coat.

MATERIALS

Pair of 2¼ mm (size 13) needles
Set of 4 double-pointed 2¼ mm (size 13) needles
2 pairs of 3¼ mm (size 10) needles
Circular 3¼ mm (size 10) needle 80 cm (31½ in) long
2 stitch holders
12 buttons

WEIGHT OF YARN AND COLOURS

Navy (A)   560 g (20 oz)
Dark Indigo blue (B)   340 g (12 oz)
Redwood pink (C1)   115 g (4 oz)
Red (C2)   115 g (4 oz)
Crimson (C3)   115 g (4 oz)
Magenta (C4)   115 g (4 oz)

MEASUREMENTS

Length from top of shoulder to bottom edge of coat: 103 cm (40½ in)
Actual width all round at underarm: 137 cm (54 in)
Sleeve length: 50 cm (19½ in)

TENSION

Over pattern, using 3¼ mm (size 10) needles, 32 stitches and 34 rows to 10 cm (4 in).

BODY CHART

Odd-numbered rows are knit, worked from right to left.
Even-numbered rows are purl, worked from left to right.

IMPORTANT

- Change shade of red of pattern every 2–3 rows to give a random effect.
- Twist wools at back of work every 1–2 stitches to avoid making holes, but do not pull tight.
- When working st st using just one colour twist a spare ball of the same colour yarn across the back of work to keep the thickness of the garment even.
- This garment is knitted sideways, beginning at the left front edge and the sleeves are knitted from cuff to shoulder.
- There are 2 background colours so always check that you are using the correct colour: panels 1, 3, 5, 7 and 9 are in A and panels 2, 4, 6, 8 and 10 are in B.
- The pattern on the fronts and back is staggered, therefore begin panels 1, 3, 5, 7 and 9 at stitch 26, row 1 of the Body chart and panels 2, 4, 6, 8 and 10 at stitch 1, row 1 of the chart.
- The pattern on the sleeves is also staggered, therefore begin panels 1 and 3 at stitch 1, row 1 of the Sleeve chart and panel 2 at stitch 38, row 1.

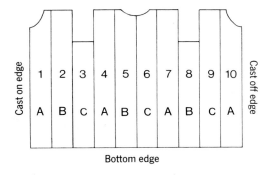

INSTRUCTIONS
FRONTS AND BACK
Panel 1

With 3¼ mm (size 10) needles and A, cast on 257 sts and work from Body chart, beg at st 26, row 1.
Rows 1–12 as chart.
Rows 13–19 inc 1 st at end (neck edge) of this and next 3 alternate rows.

Rows 20–23 inc 1 st at end (neck edge) of each row (265 sts).
Row 24 cast on 15 sts, patt to end (280 sts).
Rows 25–42 as chart, then work 4 rows rev st st in A as follows:
Row 1 k.
Row 2 k.
Row 3 p.
Row 4 k.

Panel 2

Join on B. Work from Body chart, beg at st 1, row 1.
Rows 1–41 as chart.
Pocket lining Set work on one side and with 3¼ mm (size 10) needles and B, cast on 42 sts and work 41 rows st st. Keep sts on needle. Return to main body of work and cont as follows.
Row 42 cast off 60 sts, patt 78 sts. Slip next 42 sts onto a st holder for pocket, then join on pocket lining, p from its needle, keeping to patt, and patt to end (220 sts). Then join on A and work 4 rows rev st st as before.

120 RIBBONS AND BOWS

Top of garment

Bottom of garment
SLEEVE CHART

Odd-numbered rows are knit, worked from right to left.
Even-numbered rows are purl, worked from left to right.

Panel 3 (underarm panel)
Cont in A. Work from Body chart, beg at st 26, row 1.
Rows 1–42 as chart, then work 4 rows rev st st as before.

Panel 4
Join on B. Work from Body chart, beg at st 1, row 1.
Row 1 patt to end, cast on 60 sts (280 sts).
Rows 2–42 as chart, then join on A and work 4 rows rev st st as before.

Panel 5
Cont in A. Work from Body chart, beg at st 26, row 1.
Rows 1–18 as chart.
Rows 19–23 dec 1 st at end (neck edge) of row 19 and next 2 alternate rows (277 sts).
Rows 24–42 as chart, then work 4 rows rev st st as before.

Panel 6
Join on B and work from Body chart, beg at st 1, row 1.
Rows 1–18 as chart.
Rows 19–23 inc 1 st at end (neck edge) of this and next 2 alternate rows (280 sts).
Rows 24–42 as chart, then join on A and work 4 rows rev st st as before.

Panel 7
Cont in A. Work from Body chart, beg at st 26, row 1.
Rows 1–41 as chart.
Row 42 cast off 60 sts, patt to end (220 sts), then work 4 rows rev st st as before.

Panel 8 (underarm panel)
Join on B. Work from Body chart, beg at st 1, row 1.
Rows 1–42 as chart.
Pocket top Lay work on one side and with 2¼ mm (size 13) needles and A, cast on 42 sts and work 10 rows in k1 p1 rib. P next row (to make foldline), then work 9 more rows in k1 p1 rib. Keep sts on spare needle. Return to main body of work, cont as follows.
1st row of rev st st join on A and k 100 sts. Slip sts of Pocket top onto needle and k them. Slip next 42 sts onto a st holder, then k to end. Complete panel of rev st st (k this row, p next row, k last row).

Panel 9
Cont in A. Work from Body chart, beg at st 26, row 1.
Row 1 patt to end, then cast on 60 sts (280 sts).
Rows 2–42 as chart, then work 4 rows rev st st as before.

Panel 10
Join on B. Work from Body chart, beg at st 1, row 1.

Rows 1–19 as chart.
Row 20 cast off 15 sts (neck edge) and patt to end (265 sts).
Rows 21–24 dec 1st at end (neck edge) of each row.
Rows 25–31 dec 1 st at end (neck edge) of this and next 3 alternate rows (257 sts).
Rows 32–42 as chart, then cast off loosely.

Finishing pockets

Left pocket top With wrong side facing and 3¼ mm (size 10) needles and B, slip the 42 sts from st holder onto needle and p them, then join on A and work 4 rows rev st st as before. Change to 2¼ mm (size 13) needles and work 9 rows in k1 p1 rib. K next row (to make foldline), work 9 more rows in k1 p1 rib, then cast off loosely in rib.

Right pocket lining With right side facing and 3¼ mm (size 10) needles and A, slip sts from st holder onto needle and complete border of rev st st (k next 2 rows, p next and k last row). Cont with A and work 42 rows st st. Cast off loosely.
Block (see page 155) garment and press carefully on wrong side using a damp cloth, but do not press ribbing. Stitch pocket linings in place carefully. Fold pocket tops to inside along foldline and stitch down neatly. Weave in any loose ends using a darning needle (do not just cut them off).

Shoulder seams

With 2¼ mm (size 13) needles and A, pick up and k 60 sts along right front shoulder (right side facing). Work 3 rows rev st st.

Row 1 k.
Row 2 p.
Row 3 k.

Leave sts on a spare needle.

With right side facing and 2¼ mm (size 13) needles and A, pick up and k 60 sts along right back shoulder. Leave sts on needle. Graft (see page 155) right front shoulder to right back shoulder (right sides together). Rep for left shoulder.

SLEEVES

Right sleeve

With set of 4 double-pointed 2¼ mm (size 13) needles and A, cast on 60 sts and work 36 rounds in k1 p1 rib.

Next round p (to make foldline), then work 36 more rounds in k1, p1 rib.

Inc round 1 *k1, inc into next st; rep from * to end (90 sts).

Inc round 2 inc into every st (180 sts).

Inc round 3 *k5, inc into next st; rep from * to end (210 sts).

Panel 1

Change to circular 3¼ mm (size 10) needle, join on B and work from Sleeve chart, beg at st 1, round 1.

Rounds 1–42 as chart, then join on A and work 4 rounds rev st st as follows: round 1 k; round 2 p; round 3 p; round 4 p.

Panel 2

Cont in A, beg patt at st 38, round 1 of Sleeve chart.

Rounds 1–42 as chart, then work 4 rows rev st st as before.

Panel 3

Join on B and work from Sleeve chart, beg at st 1, round 1.

Rounds 1–41 as chart.

Round 42 *k3, k2 tog; rep from * to end (168 sts), then join on A and work 4 rows rev st st as before. Cast off loosely.

Left sleeve

Work as Right sleeve, but rev colours, i.e., work panel 1 in A, panel 2 in B and panel 3 in A.

WELT

With right side facing and 2¼ mm (size 13) needles and A, pick up and k 400 sts around bottom edge of fronts and back. Work 36 rows in k1 p1 rib.

Next row k (to make foldline), then work 36 more rows in k1 p1 rib. Cast off loosely in rib. Fold welt to inside along foldline and stitch down neatly.

NECKBAND

With right side facing and 2¼ mm (size 13) needles and A, pick up and k 100 sts around neck. Work 9 rows in k1 p1 rib. Next row p (to make foldline), then work 9 more rows in k1 p1 rib. Cast off loosely in rib. Fold band to inside along foldline and stitch down neatly.

BUTTONHOLE BAND

With right side facing and 2¼ mm (size 13) needles and A, pick up and k 298 sts up right front edge.

Rows 1–4 work in k1 p1 rib, then make buttonholes.

Row 5 rib 3, cast off 6 sts, *rib 20 (counting stitch already on needle), cast off 6 sts; rep from * to last 3 sts, rib 3.

Row 6 cont in k1 p1 rib, casting on 6 sts over the 12 buttonholes.

Rows 7–9 work in k1 p1 rib.

Row 10 p (to make foldline).

Rows 11–13 work in k1 p1 rib.

Rows 14 and 15 as rows 5 and 6.

Rows 16–19 work in k1 p1 rib, then cast off loosely in rib. Fold band to inside along foldline and stitch down neatly, neatening around buttonholes with a small buttonhole st.

BUTTONBAND

With right side facing and 2¼ mm (size 13) needles and A, pick up and k 298 sts down left front edge. Work 9 rows in k1 p1 rib, p next row (to make foldline), work 9 more rows in k1 p1 rib, then cast off loosely in rib. Fold to inside along foldline and stitch down. Sew on buttons.

SLEEVE INSERTION

Press carefully on wrong side using a damp cloth, but do not press ribbing. Place sleeve in armhole with right sides tog, ensuring that centre of bow is at shoulder seam. Sew neat seam using small back sts. Weave in any loose ends using a darning needle. Fold each cuff to inside along foldline and stitch down neatly.

RUFFLED BAND

MATERIALS

Pair of 3¼ mm (size 10) needles
Pair of 4½ mm (size 7) needles
Approximately 100 by 10 cm (3 ft 4 in by 4 in) strip of 115 g (4oz) polyester wadding

WEIGHT OF YARN AND COLOURS

PLIED YARN   (or 2 strands of ordinary yarn knitted together)
Navy (A)   115 g (4 oz)
UNPLIED YARN   (for frills)
Reds (B)   14 g (½ oz)
Medium Indigo blue (C)   14 g (½ oz)
Navy (D)   14 g (½ oz)

TENSION

Over stocking stitch, using 4½ mm (size 7) needles 25 stitches and 24 rows to 10 cm (4 in).

INSTRUCTIONS

BAND

With 4½ mm (size 7) needles and A, cast on 100 sts.

Rows 1–16 work in st st.

Row 17 k, looping short strands of B at each end of row as markers.

Rows 18–22 work in st st.

Row 23 k, looping short strands of D at each end of row as markers.

Rows 24–28 work in st st.

Row 29 k, looping short strands of C at each end of row as markers.

Rows 30–34 work in st st.

Row 35 k, looping short strands of B at each end of row as markers.

Rows 36–40 work in st st.

Row 41 k, looping short strands of D at each end of row as markers.

Rows 42–46 work in st st.

Row 47 k, looping short strands of C at each end of row as markers.

Rows 48–64 work in st st, then cast off loosely. Weave in any loose ends using a darning needle (do not just cut them off) and press carefully on wrong side using a damp cloth.

FRILLS

With right side facing and 3¼ mm (size 10) needles and B, pick up and k 100 sts along row indicated by 1st markers in B.

Row 1 p.

Row 2 k, inc into every st (200 sts).

Rows 3–6 work in st st, then cast off loosely purlwise. Rep, working a frill along each row indicated by markers in same colour wool as markers.

FINISHING

Lay band (wrong side up) on a flat surface and lay strip of wadding down the centre. Bring each side of band up over wadding to meet along centre and oversew edges neatly in A. Then bring ends of band tog to form a circle and stitch ends of wadding tog, then oversew edges of ends of Band tog. To neaten, stitch edges of ends of each frill tog using very small stitches.

FIREWORKS

Names like 'bright busters', 'Prince of Wales plumes', 'flying dragons' and 'devil among the tailors' were given to old English fireworks that are no longer made. Interestingly, two of the four have a reference to clothing, and for me this design is an attempt to make a jacket look like a firework display. I studied the patterns they made, then tried to translate it onto paper without losing the sense of explosion and movement. The end result is fun to knit because the patterning uses plenty of colours and leaves the knitter free to vary the combinations. The red, pink and elderberry background is unusual, and looks awful in anything but natural dyes. The ribs are picked up after the main bulk of the knitting has been completed. If it is properly woven, the patterning should be visible from the inside as well as the outside.

MATERIALS

Pair of 2¼ mm (size 13) needles
Set of 4 double-pointed 2¼ mm (size 13) needles
2 pairs of 3¼ mm (size 10) needles
2 stitch holders
7 buttons

WEIGHT OF YARN AND COLOURS

Red (A)   230 g (8 oz)
Elderberry (B)   280 g (10 oz)
Pink (C)   170 g (6 oz)
Walnut (D1)   57 g (2 oz)
Pale walnut (D2)   57 g (2 oz)
Grey (D3)   57 g (2 oz)
Natural (D4)   57 g (2 oz)
Grape (D5)   57 g (2 oz)

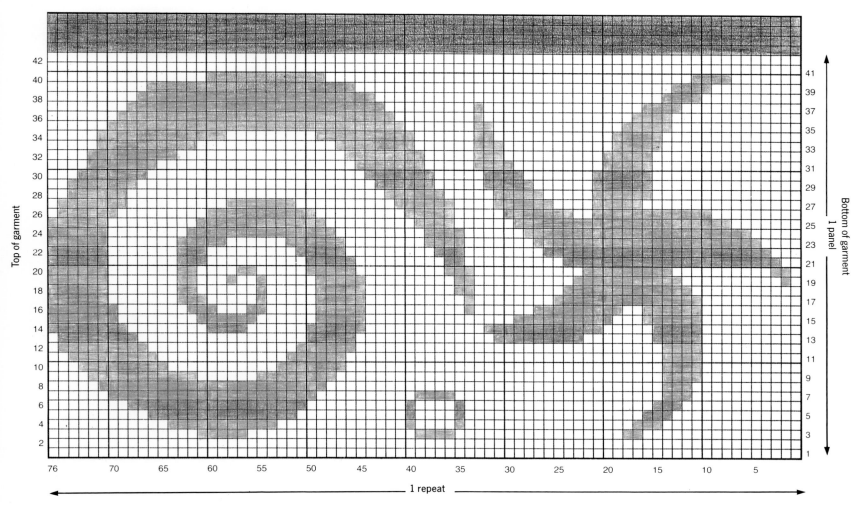

1 repeat

Odd-numbered rows are knit, worked from right to left.
Even-numbered rows are purl, worked from left to right.

MEASUREMENTS

Length from top of shoulder to bottom edge of jacket:
82.5 cm (32½ in)
Actual width all round at underarm: 142 cm (56 in)
Sleeve length: 60 cm (23½ in)

TENSION

Over pattern, using 3¼ mm (size 10) needles, 28
stitches and 30 rows to 10 cm (4 in).

IMPORTANT

● Change colours of firework motif every 2–3 rows to
give a random effect, using D shades.
● Twist wools at back of work every 2–3 sts to avoid
making holes, but do not pull tight.
● When working st st using just one colour twist a
spare ball of the same colour yarn across the back of
work to keep the thickness of the garment even.
● This garment is knitted sideways, beginning at left
front edge, and the sleeves are also knitted sideways.

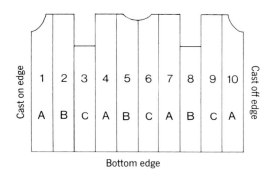

● There are 3 background colours so always check
that you are using the correct colour: panels 1, 4, 7 and
10 are in A, panels 2, 5 and 8 are in B and panels 3, 6
and 9 are in C.
● The pattern throughout is staggered, so begin panels
1, 3, 5, 7 and 9 at stitch 1 of the chart and panels 2, 4,
6, 8 and 10 at stitch 41.

INSTRUCTIONS
FRONTS AND BACK

Panel 1

With 3¼ mm (size 10) needles and A, cast on 172 sts
and work from chart, beg at st 1, row 1.

Rows 1–12 as chart.

Rows 13 With right side facing inc 1 st at end (neck
edge) of row.

Rows 14–16 as chart.

Rows 17–29 inc 1 st at end (neck edge) of 17th row
and next 6 alternate rows.

Rows 30 and 31 as chart.

Row 32 With wrong side facing cast on 15 sts, patt to
end (195 sts).

Rows 33–42 as chart, then join on B and work 4 rows
rev st st as follows:

Row 1 k.

Row 2 k.

Row 3 p.

Row 4 k.

Panel 2

Cont in B and work from chart, beg at st 41, row 1 of chart.

Rows 1–41 as chart.

Row 42 Cast off 52 sts (for armhole), patt to end (143 sts). Work 4 rows rev st st as before.

Pocket lining Lay work on one side and with 2nd pair of 3¼ mm (size 10) needles and B, cast on 42 sts and work rows 1–42 of chart, beg at st 65, row 1. Keep sts on needle.

Return to main body of work and cont as follows:

Panel 3 (underarm panel)

Join on C and work from chart, beg at st 1, row 1.

Row 1 Patt 24, slip next 42 sts onto a st holder. Join on pocket lining, k from its needle, then patt to end.

Rows 1–42 as chart, then join on B and work 4 rows rev st st as before.

Panel 4

Join on A and work from chart, beg at st 41, row 1.

Row 1 With right side facing patt to end, then cast on 52 sts (195 sts).

Rows 2–42 as chart, then join on B and work 4 rows rev st st as before.

Panel 5

Cont in B and work from chart, beg at st 1, row 1.

Rows 1–10 as chart.

Rows 11–15 dec 1 st at end (neck edge) of 11th row and next 2 alternate rows (192 sts).

Rows 16–42 as chart, then work 4 rows rev st st as before.

Panel 6

Join on C and work from chart, beg at st 41, row 1.

Rows 1–26 as chart.

Rows 27–31 inc 1 st at end (neck edge) of 27th row and next 2 alternate rows (195 sts).

Rows 32–42 as chart, then join on B and work 4 rows rev st st as before.

Panel 7

Join on A and work from chart, beg at st 1, row 1.

Rows 1–41 as chart.

Row 42 With wrong side facing cast off 52 sts, patt to end (143 sts), then join on B and work 4 rows rev st st as before.

Panel 8 (underarm panel)

Cont in B and work from chart, beg at st 41, row 1.

Rows 1–42 as chart.

Pocket top Lay work on one side and with 2¼ mm (size 13) needles and B, cast on 42 sts and work 6 rows in k1 p1 rib.

Keep sts on a spare needle.

Return to main body of work and cont as follows:

1st row of rev st st cont in B and k 24 sts. Slip sts of Pocket top onto needle and k them. Slip next 42 sts

onto a st holder, then k to end. Complete panel of rev st st (k this row, p next row, k last row).

Panel 9

Join on C and work from chart, beg at st 1, row 1.

Row 1 With right side facing patt to end, then cast on 52 sts (195 sts).

Rows 2–42 as chart, then join on B and work 4 rows rev st st as before.

Panel 10

Join on A and work from chart, beg at st 41, row 1.

Rows 1–11 as chart.

Row 12 With wrong side facing cast off 15 sts (neck edge), patt to end (180 sts).

Rows 13 and 14 as chart.

Rows 15–27 dec 1 st at end (neck edge) of row 15 and next 6 alternate rows (173 sts).

Rows 28–30 as chart.

Row 31 dec 1 st at end (neck edge) of row (172 sts).

Rows 32–42 as chart, then cast off loosely.

Finishing pockets

Left pocket top With right side facing and 2¼ mm (size 13) needles and B, slip the 42 sts from st holder onto needle and work 6 rows in k1 p1 rib, then cast off loosely in rib.

Right pocket lining With right side facing and 3¼ mm (size 10) needles and C, slip sts from st holder onto needle, and work from chart, beg at st 25, row 1, working rows 1–42 as chart, then cast off loosely. Block (see page 155) garment and press carefully on wrong side using a damp cloth, but do not press ribbing. Stitch Pocket linings and edges of Pocket tops in place carefully and weave in any loose ends using a darning needle (do not just cut them off).

Shoulder seams

With right side facing and 2¼ mm (size 13) needles and B, pick up and k 52 sts along right front shoulder. Work 3 rows rev st st as follows:

Row 1 k.

Row 2 p.

Row 3 k.

Leave sts on a spare needle.

With 2¼ mm (size 13) needles and B, pick up and k 52 sts along right back shoulder (right sides facing). Leave sts on needle. Graft (see page 155) right front shoulder to right back shoulder (right sides together). Rep for left shoulder.

SLEEVES

With 3¼ mm (size 10) needles and A, cast on 123 sts. Work 4 panels from chart in order A, B, C, B, beg at st 1 or 41, row 1 as before, with 4 rows rev st st in B between each panel and end with 4 rows rev st st in B. Leave sts on needle. Graft (see page 155) sts on needle to sts of cast on edge (right sides together). Weave in any loose ends using a darning needle (do not just cut

them off), then press carefully. Rep for 2nd sleeve.

Cuffs

With right side facing and set of 4 double-pointed 2¼ mm (size 13) needles and B, pick up and k 160 sts along lower edge of sleeve, ensuring patt is right way up.

Dec round 1 *k2 tog; rep to end (80 sts).

Dec round 2 *k2, k2 tog; rep from * to end (60 sts), then work 36 more rounds in k1 p1 rib. Join on 2nd strand B and cast off loosely in rib.

WELT

With right side facing and 2¼ mm (size 13) needles and B, pick up and k 350 sts along lower edge of fronts and back (right side facing). Work 36 rows in k1 p1 rib. Join on 2nd strand B and cast off loosely in rib.

NECKBAND

With right side facing and 2¼ mm (size 13) needles and B, pick up and k 110 sts around neck. Work 9 rows in k1 p1 rib. P next row (to make foldline), then work 9 more rows in k1 p1 rib and cast off loosely in rib. Fold band to inside along foldline and stitch down neatly.

BUTTONHOLE BAND

With right side facing and 2¼ mm (size 13) needles and B, pick up and k 218 sts up right front edge.

Rows 1–4 work in k1 p1 rib, then make buttonholes.

Row 5 rib 4, cast off 6, *rib 28 (including st on needle), cast off 6; rep from * to last 4 sts, rib 4.

Row 6 cont in k1 p1 rib, casting on 6 sts over the 7 buttonholes.

Rows 7–9 work in k1 p1 rib.

Row 10 p (to make foldline).

Rows 11–13 work in k1 p1 rib.

Rows 14 and 15 as rows 5 and 6.

Rows 16–19 work in k1 p1 rib, then cast off loosely in rib. Fold band to inside along foldline and stitch down neatly, neatening around buttonholes using a small buttonhole st.

BUTTONBAND

With right side facing and 2¼ mm (size 13) needles and B, pick up and k 218 sts down left front edge. Work 9 rows in k1 p1 rib, p next row (to make foldline), work 9 more rows in k1 p1 rib, then cast off loosely in rib. Fold band to inside along foldline and stitch down neatly. Sew on buttons.

SLEEVE INSERTION

With right side facing and set of 4 double-pointed 2¼ mm (size 13) needles and B, pick up and k 132 sts around top edge of sleeve. Work 3 rounds in p, then cast off loosely knitwise. Rep for 2nd sleeve.

Place sleeves in armholes with right sides tog, taking care to match underarm panels. Sew neat seams using small back sts. Weave in any rem loose ends using a darning needle.

SUNFLOWER

When the painter Vincent van Gogh moved to Arles in the south of France in 1888, he immediately painted his house yellow and decorated it with six pictures of sunflowers. To van Gogh, yellow was the colour of the sun, the symbol of light and warmth, and he intended his sunflowers to have the effect of a stained glass window in a medieval church, to glow with and enrich the light. This jacket is my homage to van Gogh, particularly his brave use of colour. I have tried to follow his example by using the madder as a background and giving both leaves and flowers the texture of paint, by using several tones of yellow and green. It is vital that you knit the tension square before embarking on the jacket. Carry the yarns not in use loosely across the back of the knitting by twisting them on every two to three stitches.

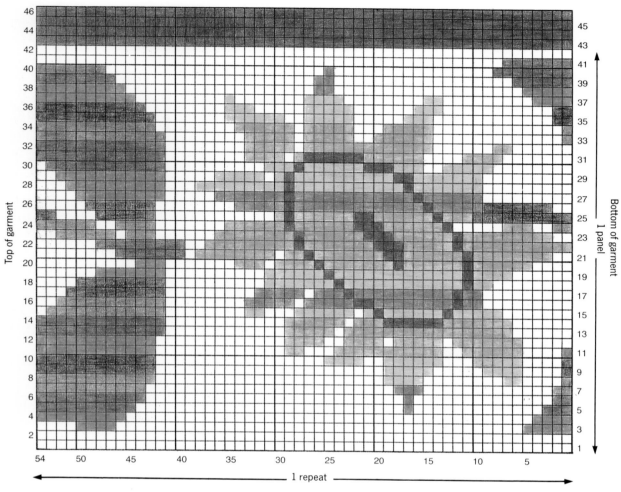

Odd-numbered rows are knit, worked from right to left.   Even-numbered rows are purl, worked from left to right.

MATERIALS
Pair of 2¼ mm (size 13) needles
Set of 4 double-pointed 2¼ mm (size 13) needles
2 pairs of 3¼ mm (size 10) needles
2 stitch holders
7 buttons

WEIGHT OF YARN AND COLOURS
Madder (A)   675 g (24 oz)
Olive green (B1)   85 g (3 oz)
Blue green (B2)   85 g (3 oz)
Grass green (B3)   85 g (3 oz)
Primrose (C1)   57 g (2 oz)
Yellow (C2)   57 g (2 oz)
Buttercup yellow (C3)   57 g (2 oz)
Ochre (D)   57 g (2 oz)

MEASUREMENTS
Length from top of shoulder to bottom edge of jacket:
76 cm (30 in)
Actual width all round at underarm: 150 cm (59 in)
Sleeve length: 53 cm (21 in)

TENSION
Over pattern, using 3¼ mm (size 10) needles, 28
stitches and 28 rows to 10 cm (4 in)

IMPORTANT
● Change the yellow of the sunflowers and green of
the leaves and stems every 2–3 rows to give a random
effect.
● Twist wools at back of work every 2–3 stitches to
avoid making holes, but do not pull tight.
● When working st st using just one colour twist a
spare ball of the same colour yarn across the back of
work to keep the thickness of the garment even.
● This garment is knitted sideways, beginning at left
front edge, and the sleeves are also knitted sideways.
● The pattern throughout is staggered, so begin panels
1, 3, 5, 7 and 9 at stitch 49 of the chart and panels 2,
4, 6, 8 and 10 at stitch 17.

INSTRUCTIONS
FRONTS AND BACK

Panel 1
With 3¼ mm (size 10) needles and A, cast on 172 sts
and work from chart, beg at st 49, row 1, working
sunflowers in shades of C and leaves and stems in
shades of B in random numbers of rows. Use D for
centre and outer ring of flowers.
Rows 1–12 as chart.
Row 13 With right side facing inc 1 st at end (neck
edge) of row.
Rows 14–16 as chart.
Rows 17–29 inc 1 st at end (neck edge) of 17th row
and next 6 alternate rows.
Rows 30 and 31 as chart.
Row 32 cast on 15 sts, patt to end (195 sts).
Rows 33–42 as chart, then join on B1 and work 4 rows
rev st st as follows:
Row 1 k.
Row 2 k.
Row 3 p.
Row 4 k.

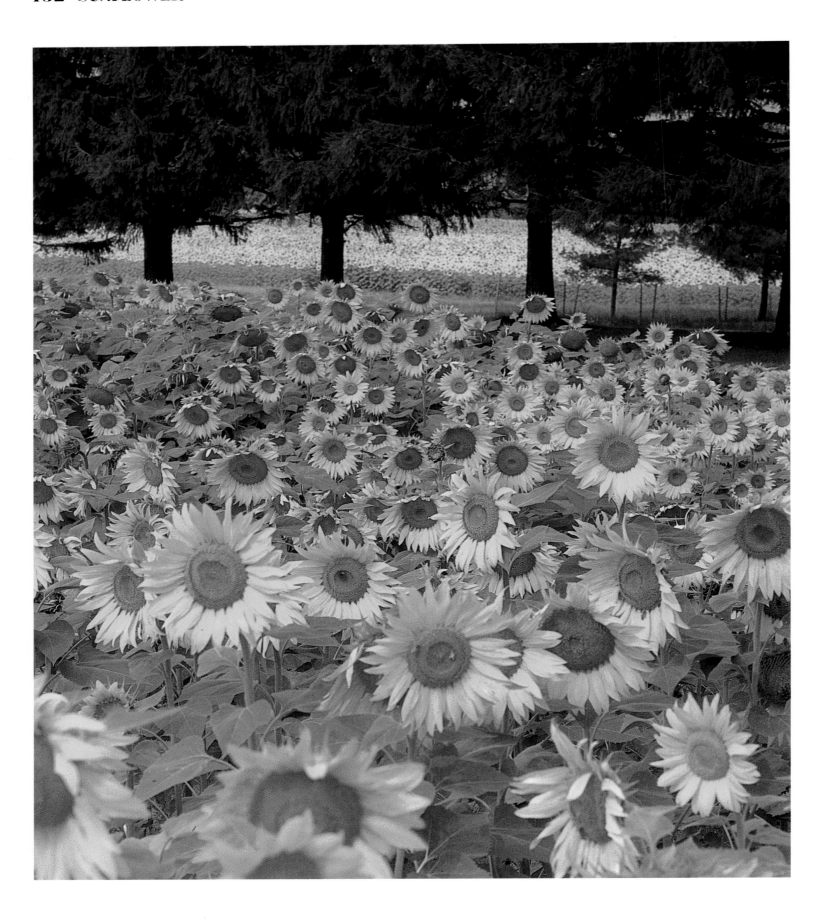

Panel 2

Join on A and work from chart, beg at st 17, row 1.
Rows 1–41 as chart.
Row 42 Cast off 52 sts, patt to end (143 sts). Work 4 rows rev st st as before.
Pocket lining Lay work on one side and with 2nd pair of 3¼ mm (size 10) needles and A, cast on 42 sts and work rows 1–42 of chart, beg at st 38, row 1. Keep sts on needle.
Return to main body of work and cont as follows.

Panel 3 (underarm panel)

Join on A and work from chart, beg at st 49, row 1.
Row 1 Patt 24, slip next 42 sts onto a st holder, then join on Pocket lining, k from its needle, and patt to end.
Rows 2–42 as chart, then join on B1 and work 4 rows rev st st as before.

Panel 4

Join on A and work from chart, beg at st 17, row 1.
Row 1 With right side facing patt to end, then cast on 52 sts (195 sts).
Rows 2–42 as chart, then join on B1 and work 4 rows rev st st as before.

Panel 5

Join on A and work from chart, beg at st 49, row 1.
Rows 1–10 as chart.
Rows 11–15 dec 1 st at end (neck edge) of 11th row and next 2 alternate rows (192 sts).
Rows 16–42 as chart, then join on B1 and work 4 rows rev st st as before.

Panel 6

Join on A and work from chart, beg at st 17, row 1.
Rows 1–26 as chart.
Rows 27–31 inc 1 st at end (neck edge) of 27th row and next 2 alternate rows (195 sts).
Rows 32–42 as chart, then join on B1 and work 4 rows rev st st as before.

Panel 7

Join on A and work from chart, beg at st 49, row 1.
Rows 1–41 as chart.
Row 42 With wrong side facing cast off 52 sts, patt to end (143 sts), then join on B1 and work 4 rows rev st st as before.

Panel 8 (underarm panel)

Join on A and work from chart, beg at st 17, row 1.
Rows 1–42 as chart.
Pocket top Lay work on one side and with 2¼ mm (size 13) needles and B1, cast on 42 sts and work 2 rows in k1 p1 rib, join on A and work 4 more rows in rib. Keep sts on spare needle. Return to main body of work and cont as follows:
1st row of rev st st join on B1 and k 24 sts. Slip sts of Pocket top onto needle and k them. Slip next 42 sts onto a st holder, then k to end. Complete panel of rev st st (k this row, p next, k last row).

Panel 9

Join on A and work from chart, beg at st 49, row 1.
Row 1 With right side facing patt to end, then cast on 52 sts (195 sts).
Rows 2–42 as chart, then join on B and work 4 rows rev st st as before.

Panel 10

Join on A and work from chart, beg at st 17, row 1.
Rows 1–11 as chart.
Row 12 With wrong side facing cast off 15 sts (neck edge), patt to end (180 sts).
Rows 13 and 14 as chart.
Rows 15–27 dec 1 st at end (neck edge) of 15th row and next 6 alternate rows (173 sts).
Rows 28–30 as chart.
Row 31 dec 1 st at end (neck edge) of row (172 sts).
Rows 32–42 as chart, then cast off loosely.
Weave in any loose ends using a darning needle (do not just cut them off). Block (see page 155) garment and press carefully on wrong side using a damp cloth, but do not press ribbing.

Finishing pockets

Right pocket lining With right side facing and 3¼ mm (size 10) needles and A, slip sts from st holder onto needle, join on A and work from chart, beg at st 17, row 1, working rows 1–42 as chart then cast off loosely.
Left pocket top With right side facing and 2¼ mm (size 13) needles and A, slip the 42 sts from st holder onto needle and work 4 rows in k1 p1 rib.
Join on B1 and work 2 rows in rib, then cast off loosely in rib. Stitch Pocket linings and edges of Pocket tops in place carefully. Weave in any loose ends using a darning needle (do not just cut them off).

Shoulder seams

With right side facing and 2¼ mm (size 13) needles and B1, pick up and k 52 sts along right front shoulder. Work 3 rows rev st st as follows:
Row 1 k.
Row 2 p.
Row 3 k.
Leave sts on spare needle.
With right side facing and 2¼ mm (size 13) needles and B1, pick up and k 52 sts along right back shoulder. Leave sts on needle. Graft (see page 155) right front shoulder to right back shoulder (right sides together). Rep for left shoulder.

SLEEVES

With 3¼ mm (size 10) needles and A, cast on 123 sts and work 4 panels from chart, beg at st 49 or 17, row 1 as before, with 4 rows rev st st in B1 between each panel and end with 4 rows rev st st in B1. Leave sts on needle. Press carefully on wrong side using a damp cloth. Graft (see page 155) sts on needle to sts of cast on edge (right sides together). Weave in any loose ends using a darning needle (do not just cut them off). Rep for 2nd sleeve.

Cuffs

With right side facing and set of 4 double-pointed 2¼ mm (size 13) needles and A, pick up and k 122 sts along lower edge of sleeve, ensuring patt is right way up.
Dec round 1 *k2 tog; rep from * to end (61 sts).
Dec round 2 *k4, k2 tog; rep from * to last 7 sts, k4, k3 tog (50 sts), then work 36 rounds in k1 p1 rib. Join on B1 and work 2 rounds in k1 p1 rib, join on 2nd strand B1 and cast off loosely in rib.

WELT

With right side facing and 2¼ mm (size 13) needles and A, pick up and k 350 sts along lower edge of fronts and back. Work 35 rows in k1 p1 rib, join on B1 and work 2 rows in rib, join on 2nd strand B1, then cast off loosely in rib.

NECKBAND

With right side facing and 2¼ mm (size 13) needles and A, pick up and k 110 sts around neck, beg at right front neck edge. Work 9 rows in k1 p1 rib. P next row (to make foldline), then work 9 more rows in k1 p1 rib and cast off loosely in rib. Fold band to inside along foldline and stitch down neatly.

BUTTONHOLE BAND

With right side facing and 2¼ mm (size 13) needles and A, pick up and k 218 sts up right front edge.
Rows 1–4 work in k1 p1 rib, then make buttonholes.
Row 5 rib 4 sts, cast off 6, *rib 28 (including st on needle), cast off 6; rep from * to last 4 sts, rib 4.
Row 6 cont in k1 p1 rib, casting on 6 sts over the 7 buttonholes.
Rows 7–9 work in k1 p1 rib.
Row 10 p (to make foldline).
Rows 11–13 work in k1 p1 rib.
Rows 14 and 15 as rows 5 and 6.
Rows 16–19 work in k1 p1 rib, then cast off loosely in rib. Fold band to inside along foldline and stitch down neatly, neatening around buttonholes using a small buttonhole st.

BUTTONBAND

With right side facing and 2¼ mm (size 13) needles and A, pick up and k 218 sts down left front edge. Work 9 rows in k1 p1 rib, p next row (to make foldline), work 9 more rows in k1 p1 rib, then cast off loosely in rib. Fold band to inside along foldline and stitch down neatly. Sew on buttons.

SLEEVE INSERTION

With right side facing and set of 4 double-pointed 2¼ mm (size 13) needles and B1, pick up and k 132 sts around top edge of sleeve. Work 3 rounds in p, then cast off loosely knitwise.
Place sleeves in armholes with right sides tog. Sew neat seams using small back sts. Weave in any rem loose ends using a darning needle.

HIGHWAYMAN

This jacket marks my most radical departure from traditional Fair Isle design, yet it gives the impression of being a tailored jacket. The highwayman remains a flamboyant figure of legend, and I have given the jacket the huge dramatic sleeves of many of the ballet costumes designed for Diaghilev's *Ballets Russes.* The quality of the knitting is all important, and the tension needs to be perfect if the final jacket is to hang properly.

MATERIALS
Pair of 2¼ mm (size 13) needles
Set of 4 double-pointed 2¼ mm (size 13) needles
Circular 2¼ mm (size 13) needle 40 cm (16 in) long
Pair of 3¼ mm (size 10) needles
7 stitch holders
8 buttons
8 press fasteners

WEIGHT OF YARN AND COLOURS
Natural (A)   200 g (7 oz)
Dark grey (B)   310 g (11 oz)
Redwood pink (C)   370 g (13 oz)

MEASUREMENTS
Length from top of shoulder to bottom edge of jacket:
76 cm (30 in)
Actual width all round at underarm: 96.5 cm (38 in)
Sleeve length: 42 cm (16½ in)

TENSION
Over check and moss stitch pattern, using 3¼ mm (size 10) needles. 32 sts and 36 rows to 10 cm (4 in).

CHART 1
Top of garment

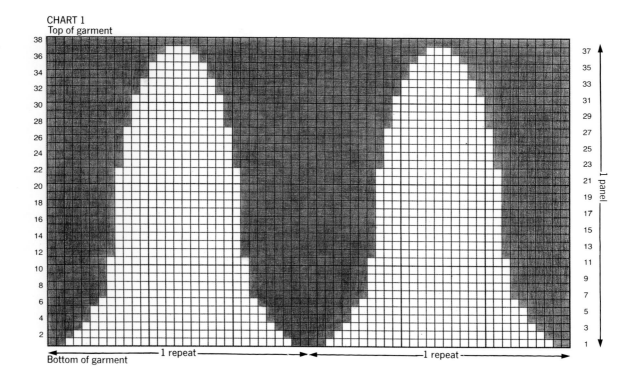

Bottom of garment — 1 repeat — — 1 repeat —

1 panel

IMPORTANT

- Twist wools at back of work every 1–2 stitches to avoid making holes, but do not pull tight.
- Take care to keep check pattern in 'draughtboard' sequence throughout.
- When you are working in st st using just one colour twist a spare ball of the same colour yarn across the back of work to keep the thickness of the garment even.
- When changing the yarn colour and working in moss st, always knit the first row on the right side to avoid colour 'pips'.

INSTRUCTIONS
FRONTS AND BACK
Peplum

Right half **With 3¼ mm (size 10) needles and A, cast on 186 sts and work 6 rows in st st. Join on B and work rows 1–38 as chart 1. With right side facing cont in B only as follows:

Next row k14, k3 tog, *k28, k3 tog; rep from * to last 14 sts, k to end (174 sts). Then work 15 more rows in st st, beg with p row.

Next row k2, *k2 tog, k15; rep from * to last 2 sts, k2 (164 sts).

Next row p. Cut off B, join on C, then k2 tog, k to last 2 sts, k2 tog (162 sts). Then work 7 rows in m st. Cut off C**. Join on A and B and work 12 rows in check patt from chart 2, beg row 1 with k6 in B (right side facing). Cut off A and B. ***Join on 2 strands C, change to 2¼ mm (size 13) needles and cont as follows:

Next row *k1, k2 tog; rep from * to end (108 sts).

Work 16 rows in k1 p1 rib.

Next row rib 9, *rib 2, inc into next st; rep from * to last 9 sts, rib 9 (138 sts). Cut off both strands C***.
Change back to 3¼ mm (size 10) needles and join on A and B. Keeping checks correct, work 6 rows of check patt from chart 2, inc 1 st at edge of back on every row (i.e., end of rows 1, 3 and 5 and beg of rows 2, 4 and 6; 144 sts). Leave sts on a spare needle.

Left half Work as given for Right half from ** to **, then cont as follows: work 12 rows check patt from chart 2, beg with k6 in A. Cut off A and B, then work as given for Right half from *** to ***. Then change back to 3¼ mm (size 10) needles and, keeping checks correct, work 6 rows of check patt from chart 2, inc 1 st at edge of back on every row (i.e., beg of rows 1, 3 and 5 and end rows 2, 4 and 6; 144 sts). Leave sts on needle.

Joining 2 halves together With 3¼ mm (size 10) needles and A and B, keeping checks correct, patt the 144 sts of Right half and then the 144 sts of Left half, making sure that the back edges are tog (288 sts).

Waist to armholes

Work 5 rows from chart 2 to complete check patt, then cut off A and B and join on C.

Next row k (to avoid colour 'pips'). Work 7 rows in m st, then cut off C. Join on A and B and work 12 rows check patt from chart 2, then cut off A and B and join on C. Work 8 rows in m st, then cut off C and join on A and B. Work 12 rows check patt from chart 2, cut off A and B and join on C. Work 8 rows in m st, then cut off C.

Odd-numbered rows are knit, worked from right to left (except the moss st panel).

Even-numbered rows are purl, worked from left to right (except the moss st panel).

CHART 2

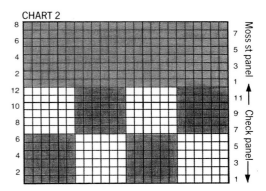

Moss st panel

Check panel

Divide for fronts and back

With right side facing join on A and B and patt 54 sts, keeping checks correct, then join on small ball of C and work 10 sts in m st (64 sts), then turn. Keeping 10 st border of m st in C at armhole edge, work on these sts as follows:

Next 11 rows work in A and B in check patt from chart 2.

Next 8 rows work in C in m st.

Next 12 rows work in A and B in check patt from chart 2.

CHART 3

St 20 is 1st st for cuff.

Next 8 rows work in C in m st.
Rep these last 20 rows once, then work 12 rows in A and B in check patt from chart 2 and 2 rows in C in m st.

Neck shaping
With right side facing cast off 16 sts, m st to end.
Next row m st.
Next row k2 tog, m st to end.
Next row m st.
Rep last 2 rows once, then cut off C (46 sts).
Join on A and B and, keeping 10 st border of m st at armhole edge, work 12 rows check patt from chart 2 decreasing 1 st at neck edge on first and each alternate row until 40 sts rem. Cut off A and B. Join on C and work 6 rows m st. Slip sts onto a st holder for right front shoulder. Slip next 16 sts onto a st holder for underarm. Join on C and work 10 sts in m st. Join on A and B and work 108 sts in check patt from chart 2, beg with k6 in A. Join on another small ball of C and work 10 more sts in m st (128 sts). Work on these sts for back. Keeping 10 sts at each end of row worked in C in m st, work straight as chart 2 as follows:
Next 11 rows work in A and B in check patt from chart 2.
Next 8 rows work in C in m st.
Next 12 rows work in A and B in check patt from chart 2.
Next 8 rows work in C in m st.
Rep these last 20 rows twice, then work 12 rows in A and B in check patt from chart 2 and 2 rows in C in m st.
Next row m st 42 sts (right side facing), k2 tog, turn.
Next row k2 tog, m st to end.

Next row m st to last 2 sts, k2 tog.
Next row k2 tog, m st to end (40 sts), then slip sts onto a st holder for right back shoulder.
With right side facing slip next 40 sts onto a st holder for back neck, then work rem 44 sts as follows in C:
Next row k2 tog, patt to end.
Next row patt to last 2 sts, k2 tog.
Rep these 2 rows once (40 sts), then slip sts onto a st holder for left back shoulder. Slip next 16 sts onto a st holder for underarm then work rem 64 sts. Join on C and m st 10 sts, then join on A and B and work 54 sts in check patt from chart 2, keeping 10 st border of m st at armhole edge. Cont as follows:
Next 11 rows work in A and B in check patt from chart 2.
Next 8 rows work in C in m st.
Next 12 rows work in A and B in check patt from chart 2.
Next 8 rows work in C in m st.
Rep these last 20 rows once, then work 12 rows in A and B in check patt from chart 2 and 1 row in C in m st.
Next row With wrong side facing cast off 16 sts, m st to end.
Next row m st.
Next row k2 tog, m st to end.
Rep last 2 rows twice and then cut off C (45 sts).
Join on A and B and, keeping 10 st border of m st at armhole edge, work 10 rows check patt from chart 2 decreasing 1 st at neck edge on every alternate row until 40 sts rem. Work final 2 rows check patt, then cut off A and B. Join on C and work 6 rows m st. Slip these sts onto a st holder. Weave in any loose ends using a darning needle. Block (see page 155) garment and press carefully on wrong side using a damp cloth.

Shoulder seams
Graft (see page 155) right front shoulder to right back shoulder (right sides together). Rep for other shoulder.

Finishing centre back vent
Left side With right side facing and 2¼ mm (size 13) needles and 2 strands C, pick up and k 38 sts from bottom of vent to beg of 1st m st band and 25 sts from there to top of ribbed waist (63 sts). Then work 5 rows m st, inc 1 st at shaped edge of vent on every row (68 sts).
Next row cast off 56 sts in m st (right side facing), leaving rem 12 sts on a spare needle.
Right side With 2¼ mm (size 13) needles and 2 strands C, pick up and k 25 sts from top of ribbed waist to bottom of 1st band of m st and 38 sts from there to end of vent (63 sts). Then work 5 rows m st, inc 1 st at shaped edge of vent on every row (68 sts) and leave sts on needle. Graft (see page 155) 12 sts on spare needle for left side of vent to matching 12 sts on needle for right side of vent (right sides facing). Cast off rem 56 sts of right side of vent. Top st increased edges of m st to vent of garment neatly.

Finishing front edges
Right edge With right side facing and 2¼ mm (size 13) needles and 2 strands C, pick up and k 142 sts between bottom edge of peplum and neck edge. Work 6 rows m st, then cast off loosely in m st.
Left edge Work as Right edge, but pick up sts from neck edge to bottom edge.

Finishing bottom edges of peplum
With right side facing and 2¼ mm (size 13) needles and 2 strands C, pick up and k 164 sts along bottom edge of right side. Work 6 rows m st, then cast off loosely in m st. Rep for left side. Weave in any loose ends using a darning needle (do not just cut them off), then press carefully on wrong side using a damp cloth.

COLLAR
Important When working collar, its right side will be facing you when wrong side of fronts and backs are facing, but this is so that when it is folded back on finished garment, its right side is uppermost.
With right side facing and 2¼ mm (size 13) needles and 2 strands C, beg at inner edge of right front band and pick up and k 32 sts up right front neck edge, rib 40 sts on st holder at back of neck, then pick up and k 32 sts down left front neck edge to inner edge of left front band (104 sts). Cont with 2 strands C.
Next row m st 6, work in k1 p1 rib to last 6 sts, m st 6. Rep this row 6 more times.
Next row m st 6, p2 tog, *rib 8, p2 tog; rep from * to last 6 sts, m st 6 (94 sts).
Next row m st 6 in C, join on b (use single strand, but twist in another ball of B at back to maintain even thickness) and k to last 6 sts. Join on small ball of C, m st 6 in C.

Next row m st 6 in C, p to last 6 sts in B, m st 6 in C. Rep these last 2 rows twice.

Next row m st 6 in C, in B, k1, *inc into next st, k7; rep from * to last 7 sts, k1, m st 6 in C (104 sts).

Next 3 rows work straight in B with m st borders in C at each end.

Next row m st 6 in C, in B, k2, *k3, inc into next st; rep from * to last 8 sts, k2, m st 6 in C (126 sts).

Change to 3¼ mm (size 10) needles and work 3 rows straight in B with m st borders in C at each end.

Next row m st 6, *k2, inc into next st; rep from * to last 6 sts, m st 6 (164 sts). Then work 3 rows straight in B with m st borders in C at each end, then work from chart 3, beg at st 1, row 1 and keeping patt correct, as follows:

Row 1 m st 6 in C, in B, *patt 18, inc into next st; rep from * to last 6 sts, m st 6 in C (172 sts).

Rows 2–6 as chart.

Row 7 m st 6 in C, in A and B, k1, inc into next st, *patt 16, inc into next st, patt 2, inc into next st; rep from * to last 24 sts, k16, inc into next st, k1, m st 6 in C (188 sts).

Rows 8–16 as chart, working extra sts in A.

Row 17 m st 6 in C, in A and B, k4, inc into next st, *patt 12, inc into next st, patt 8, inc into next st; rep from * to last 23 sts, patt 12, inc into next st, patt 4, m st 6 in C (204 sts).

Rows 18–22 as chart, working extra sts in A. Cut off B. Keeping m st border at each end and with A (twisting in an extra ball of A at back of work to keep thickness even), cont as follows:

Row 23 m st 6 in C, in A, *patt 7, inc into next st; rep from * to last 6 sts, m st 6 in C (228 sts).

Rows 24–28 as chart, then cut off A.

Next 6 rows with 2 strands C, work in m st. Cast off loosely in m st.

SLEEVES

With 3¼ mm (size 10) needles and B, cast on 118 sts. Weaving in an extra ball of B at back of work, work 16 rows in st st. Cut off extra strand B.

Join on A and work rows 1–7 of chart 4, beg at st 1, row 1, then cut off B. Join on C and work rows 8–12 of chart 4 then cut off A. Cont in C and work 30 rows in st st, weaving in a 2nd ball of C at back of work, then cut off 1 strand C. Join on A and work rows 1–7 of chart 4, then cut off C. Join on B and work rows 8–12 of chart 4, then cut off A. Cont in B and work 30 rows in st st, weaving in a 2nd ball of B, then cut off 1 strand B. Rep from * to * once, then cont in B and work 16 rows in st st, weaving in an extra ball of B. Do not cast off. Press carefully on wrong side under a damp cloth. Graft (see page 155) cast on edge to sts on needle (right sides together). Weave in loose ends using a darning needle.

Cuffs

With set of 4 double-pointed 2¼ mm (size 13) needles and 2 strands C, pick up and k 112 sts around bottom edge of sleeve.

Next round *k2 tog; rep from * to end (56 sts).

Next round *k1, p1, k1, p2 tog; rep from * to last 6 sts, k1, p1, k1, p3 tog (44 sts).

Work 10 more rounds in k1 p1 rib, then cut off both strands of C. Join on B and k 1 round.

Next round k, inc into every st (88 sts).

Next round k4, *k6, inc into next st; rep from * to end (100 sts).

Join on A and, beg with st 20, row 3 of chart 3, and continuing in rounds, work rounds 3–6.

Round 7 inc into 1st st, inc into next st, *k18, inc into next st, inc into next st; rep from * to last 18 sts, k18 (110 sts).

Rounds 8–11 as chart, working extra sts in A.

Round 12 k4, inc into next st, *k16, inc into next st, k4, inc into next st; rep from * to last 17 sts, k16, inc into next st (120 sts).

Rounds 13–16 as chart.

Round 17 k6, inc into next st, *k14, inc into next st, k8, inc into next st; rep from * to last 17 sts, k14, inc into next st, k2 (130 sts).

Rounds 18–26 as chart, then cut off A and B. Join on C (single strand), and k 1 round, then work 5 rounds m st. Cast off loosely in m st. Rep for 2nd cuff.

Sleeve insertion

With sleeve folded along underarm seam, make box pleat (see page 157) in panel at top of sleeve so that centre of pleat is on foldline of sleeve and aligns with shoulder seam of jacket. With a 2¼ mm (size 13) circular needle and C, pick up and k 130 sts around top edge of sleeve. Place sleeve in armhole of jacket and, with box pleat at shoulder seam and right sides together, graft (see page 155) together, beg with the 16 sts on st holder for armhole. Rep for 2nd sleeve.

FINISHING

Weave in any rem loose ends using a darning needle, block (see page 155) garment and give a final careful press on wrong side using a damp cloth, but do not press ribbing. Sew on buttons to right front band, then sew 8 press fasteners to front bands to secure.

CHART 4

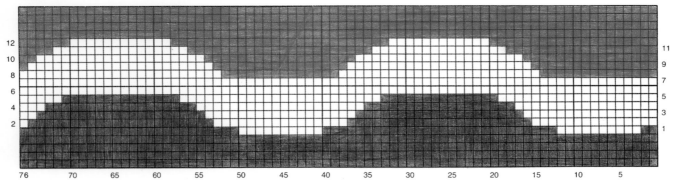

76 70 65 60 55 50 45 40 35 30 25 20 15 10 5

12 10 8 6 4 2

11 9 7 5 3 1

Odd-numbered rows are knit, worked from right to left (except the moss st panel).
Even-numbered rows are purl, worked from left to right (except the moss st panel).

AUTUMN LEAF

From the converted cow shed in which I work I can see an ancient wood. Oaks tower up, and in autumn the entire wood turns a mass of gold and russet – the colours traditionally associated with natural dyes. But used too often they can lose their impact, becoming sludgy and dull, and I have livened up the design by brightening the colours of the leaves. Natural dyes are versatile enough to make us believe that leaves really are these colours, and I enjoyed using walnuts and onion skins to dye the background. The design is knitted on circular needles, starting at the bottom rib and knitting up. This is a simple design to knit and looks gorgeous.

MATERIALS
Pair of 2¼ mm (size 13) needles
Circular 2¼ mm (size 13) needle 40 cm (16 in) long
Set of 4 double-pointed 2¼ mm (size 13) needles
Pair of 3¼ mm (size 10) needles
Circular 3¼ mm (size 10) needle 80 cm (31½ in) long
Set of 4 double-pointed 3¼ mm (size 10) needles
7 stitch holders

WEIGHT OF YARN AND COLOURS
Walnut (A)   280 g (10 oz)
Pale walnut (B)   230 g (8 oz)
Ochre (C)   170 g (6 oz)
Elderberry (D)   28 g (1 oz)
Buttercup yellow (E)   57 g (2 oz)
Navy (F)   57 g (2 oz)
Grass green (G)   57 g (2 oz)
Blue green (H)   28 g (1 oz)
Redwood pink (I)   57 g (2 oz)

MEASUREMENTS
Length from top of shoulder to bottom edge of sweater 71 cm (28 in)
Actual width all round at underarm: 106 cm (42 in)
Sleeve length: 57 cm (22½ in)

TENSION
Over pattern, using 3¼ mm (size 10) needles, 33 sts and 32 rows to 10 cm (4 in).

IMPORTANT
● Twist wools at back of work every 1–2 sts to avoid making holes, but do not pull tight.
● When working st st using just one colour twist a spare ball of the same colour yarn across the back of work to keep the thickness of the garment even.
● To make ridge on right side of work between each panel, round 2 of the chart is purl when using the circular needle and rows 1 and 2 are knit when 2 needles are being used.
● The sweater is knitted on a circular needle as far as the underarm, so every round of the chart up to that point is knit (except round 2, which is purl).
● When working in rounds for the sleeves, remember to work chart in reverse order as you are knitting from shoulder to cuff, that is, you work from round 26 to 1. Round 1 of the chart is purl.
● When using the circular needle, loop a short strand of brightly coloured wool around the first stitch each time you begin a round so that you can find the beginning easily.
● Before beginning each new panel, check with the diagram (above right) to ensure that you have the correct colour combination.

8	B
7	C
6	B
5	A
4	B
3	C
2	B
1	A

Key
A = background B, leaf 1 D, leaf 2 E
B = background A, leaf 1 F, leaf 2 G
C = background B, leaf 1 H, leaf 2 I
(The sweater in the photographs has been knitted using additional colours in an alternative combination.)
The edges of the ribbing, the stems of the leaves and rounds 1 and 2 of all panels are worked in C.
Work the 6 panels of sleeve with the colour combinations in the following order: panel 1 in B, panel 2 in C, panel 3 in B, panel 4 in A, panel 5 in B, panel 6 in C.

INSTRUCTIONS
FRONT AND BACK

With 2¼ mm (size 13) circular needle and 2 strands C, cast on 264 sts and work 2 rounds in k1 p1 rib. Join on 2 strands A and work 25 rounds in k1 p1 rib. Cont with single strand.
Inc round *k2, inc into next st; rep from * to end (352 sts).
Change to 3¼ mm (size 10) circular needle and work from chart, beg at row 2, st 1 (p in C). Work straight until 5 complete panels, with colour combinations in order A, B, C, B and A, have been worked.

Divide for front and back

Slip 1st 16 sts onto a st holder (Holder 1), then with pair of 3¼ mm (size 10) needles and C, patt 144 sts, turn. Leave rem sts on circular needle. Work straight until panels 6 and 7, using colour combinations B and C, have been worked. Then work rows 1–18 of panel 8 in colour combination B.
Row 19 patt 44 sts. K2 tog, turn.
Rows 20–26 dec 1 st at neck edge every row (38 sts).
Rows 1 and 2 as chart, then slip sts onto a st holder for shoulder. Slip next 52 sts onto a st holder for neck, then cont on rem 46 sts as follows:
Row 19 With right side facing k2 tog, patt to end.
Rows 20–26 dec 1 st at neck edge every row (38 sts).
Rows 1 and 2 as chart, then slip sts onto a st holder.
With right side facing return to rem 192 sts and slip next 32 sts onto a st holder (Holder 2). With pair of 3¼ mm (size 10) needles and colour combination B, patt 144 sts and slip rem 16 sts onto Holder 1. Work straight until panels 6 and 7, using colour combinations B and C,

have been worked. Then work rows 1–18 of panel 8 in colour combination B.
Row 19 patt 44 sts, k2 tog, turn.
Rows 20–26 dec 1 st at neck edge every row (38 sts), then slip sts onto a st holder. Slip next 52 sts onto a st holder, then cont on rem 46 sts as follows:
Row 19 k2 tog, patt to end.
Rows 20–26 dec 1 st at neck edge every row (38 sts). Leave sts on needle.

Shoulder seams

Block (see page 155) garment and press carefully on wrong side using a damp cloth. Graft (see page 155) right front shoulder to right back shoulder (right sides together). Rep for left shoulder. Weave in any loose ends using a darning needle (do not just cut them off).

SLEEVES

Remember to k all rounds (except round 1, which is p) and work panels in rev order – from round 26–1.
With 3¼ mm (size 10) circular needle and right side facing and C, slip last 16 sts from Holder 1 onto left needle and k them. Pick up and k 144 sts around armhole and then k the rem 16 sts from Holder (176 sts).

K 1 round and p 1 round in C, then work from chart, beg at st 1, round 26 of bottom panel of chart, until 6 panels have been worked, ending with round 5.
Round 4 k2, *k1, k2 tog; rep from * to end (118 sts). Change to set of 4 double-pointed 2¼ mm (size 13) needles.
Round 3 k2, *k2 tog; rep from * to end (60 sts).
Rounds 2 and 1 k 1 round and p 1 round in C. Join on 2 strands A and work 25 rounds in k1 p1 rib. Then join on 2 strands C, work 2 rounds in k1 p1 rib and cast off loosely in rib. Rep for 2nd sleeve. Weave in any loose ends using a darning needle and press carefully on wrong side using a damp cloth.

NECKBAND

With right side facing and set of 4 double-pointed 2¼ mm (size 13) needles and A, k the 52 sts for back of neck, pick up and k 20 sts down left side of neck, k the 52 sts for front of neck and then pick up and k 20 sts up right side of neck (144 sts). Work 8 rounds in k1 p1 rib. Join on C, work 2 rounds in k1 p1 rib, p 1 round, work 2 more rounds in k1 p1 rib, then join on A. Work 7 more rounds in k1 p1 rib then cast off loosely in rib. Fold band to inside along foldline and stitch down neatly.

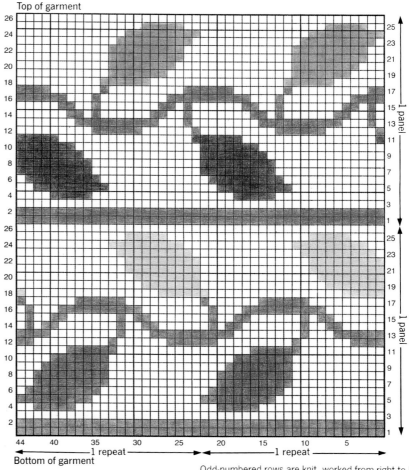

Top of garment

Bottom of garment

1 repeat — 1 repeat

Odd-numbered rows are knit, worked from right to left.
Even-numbered rows are purl, worked from left to right.

IONIC COLUMNS

I'd been wanting to design something architectural for years before finally perfecting this pattern. If nothing else, it's taught me the difference between Doric, Corinthian and Ionic columns. The ribs are Roman bricks. This is one of my favourite recent designs, simply because it is so striking – the pattern doesn't repeat, and neither the front, back nor sleeves match. Because it's so original and sophisticated, it's great fun to wear.

WEIGHT OF YARN AND COLOURS

Medium Indigo blue (A)   280 g (10 oz)
Grey (B)   230 g (8 oz)
Navy (C)   230 g (8 oz)
Pale walnut (D)   170 g (6 oz)
Burgundy (E1)   57 g (2 oz)
Madder (E2)   57 g (2 oz)
Redwood pink (E3)   57 g (2 oz)

MEASUREMENTS

Length from top of shoulder to bottom edge of jacket: 58 cm (23 in)
Actual width all round at underarm: 129.5 cm (51 in)
Sleeve length: 46 cm (18 in)

TENSION

Over pattern, using 3¼ mm (size 10) needles, 30 stitches and 30 rows to 10 cm (4 in).

IMPORTANT

● Twist wools at back of work every 1–2 sts to avoid making holes, but do not pull tight.
● This garment is knitted sideways, beginning at right front edge.
● When working the brick pattern, change colour of bricks every 2–3 rows to add texture.
● When working st st using just one colour twist a spare ball of the same colour yarn across the back of work to keep the thickness of the garment even.
● The number of rows on the shoulders and underarms varies. This is in the design of the garment so do not be concerned.

MATERIALS

Pair of 2¼ mm (size 13) needles
Set of 4 double-pointed 2¼ mm (size 13) needles
Pair of 3¼ mm (size 10) needles
Circular 3¼ mm (size 10) needle 40 cm (16 in) long
1 stitch holder
7 buttons

INSTRUCTIONS

FRONTS AND BACK

With 3¼ mm (size 10) needles and A, cast on 140 sts and, beg with k row, work 2 rows in st st. Then work from chart 1, beg at st 1, row 1.

Rows 1–6 as chart.

Rows 7 and 9 inc 1 st at beg of row (neck edge), then cont as chart but work each alternate row as follows:

Rows 11 and 13 cast on 2 sts at beg of row (neck edge).

Rows 15 and 17 cast on 3 sts at beg of row (neck edge).

Rows 19 and 21 cast on 5 sts at beg of row (neck edge; 162 sts).

Rows 22–68 as chart.

Row 69 cast off 60 sts (102 sts).

Rows 70–84 as chart.

Rows 85–95 as chart, beg row 87 with k4 in B (these rows will be referred to later as one block of bricks).

Rows 96–100 work in A.

Rows 101–112 work in A from chart 2.

Rows 113–116 as chart.

Row 117 cast on 60 sts (162 sts).

Rows 118–168 as chart.

Row 169 cast off 2 sts at beg of row (neck edge).

Row 170 as chart.

Row 171 k2 tog (neck edge), patt to end.

Rows 172–173 as chart.

Row 174 work as chart to last 2 sts, p2 tog (neck edge; 158 sts).

Rows 175–200 as chart.

Rows 201–205 work from chart 3.

Row 206 work as chart to last st, inc into last st (neck edge).

Rows 207–209 as chart.

Row 210 work as chart to last st, inc into last st (neck edge).

Rows 211 and 212 as chart.

Row 213 cast on 2 sts at beg of row (neck edge; 162 sts).

Rows 214–264 as chart.

Row 265 cast off 60 sts at beg of row (102 sts).

Rows 266–300 as chart.

Rows 301–314 work from chart 4.

Row 315 cast on 60 sts at beg of row (162 sts).

Rows 316–368 as chart.

Rows 369–371 cast off 5 sts at beg of this and next alternate row (neck edge).

Row 372 as chart.

Rows 373 and 375 cast off 3 sts at beg of row (neck edge).

Row 376 as chart.

Rows 377 and 379 cast off 2 sts at beg of row (neck edge).

Row 380 as chart.

Rows 381 and 383 cast off 1 st at beg of this and next alternate row (neck edge).

Rows 384–388 as chart, then cast off loosely. Weave in any loose ends using a darning needle (do not just cut

them off). Block (see page 155) garment and press carefully on wrong side using a damp cloth.

Shoulder seams

With right side facing and 3¼ mm (size 10) needles and B, pick up and k 51 sts along back right shoulder, then slip sts onto a st holder.

With right side facing and 3¼ mm (size 10) needles and B, pick up and k 51 sts along front right shoulder. Next row p.

Work 1 complete block of bricks (see rows 87–95, chart 1), beg row 1 with k2 in B and end with 2 rows in B. Then graft (see page 155) right front shoulder to right back shoulder (right sides together). Rep for left shoulder.

SLEEVES

Right sleeve

With 3¼ mm (size 10) needles and A, cast on 115 sts. Work from chart 5, beg at st 1, row 1 and work rows 1–164. Keep sts on needle and graft (see page 155) them to cast on edge (right sides together).

Left sleeve

Work as right sleeve, but work from chart 5 beg at st 1 row 81.

Work rows 81–164 as chart, then work rows 1–80 as chart. Keep sts on needle and graft as for right sleeve.

Cuffs

With right side facing and set of 4 double-pointed 2¼ mm (size 13) needles and A, pick up and k 132 sts (44 sts per needle) around bottom edge of sleeve.

Round 1 *k4, k2 tog; rep from * to end (110 sts).

Round 2 *k3, k2 tog; rep from * to end (88 sts).

Round 3 *k8, k2 tog; rep from * to last 8 sts, k8 (80 sts).

Rounds 4–32 join on B and work 3 complete blocks of bricks (see rows 85–93, chart 1, but remember to k every round), beg and end with 2 rows in B and working 2 rounds in B between blocks of bricks and 1 st in B between each brick.

Round 33 p (to make foldline).

Work 30 more rounds in k1 p1 rib in B, then cast off loosely in rib. Fold cuff to inside along foldline and stitch down neatly.

WELT

With right side facing and 2¼ mm (size 13) needles and B, pick up and k 371 sts along bottom edge of fronts and back. P1 row.

Rows 1–29 work 3 complete blocks of bricks (see rows 85–95, chart 1), beg and end with 2 rows in B, and beg and end each row with 2 sts in B.

Row 30 k (to make foldline).

Work 30 more rows in B in k1 p1 rib, then cast off loosely, in rib. Fold welt to inside along foldline and stitch down neatly.

NECKBAND

With right side facing and 2¼ mm (size 13) needles and B, pick up and k 131 sts around neck. P 1 row.

Rows 1–20 work 2 complete blocks of bricks (see rows 85–93, chart 1), beg and end with 2 rows in B and beg and end each row with 2 sts in B.

Row 21 p (to make foldline).

Work 2 more complete blocks of bricks (20 rows), beg and end with 2 rows in B, then cast off loosely. Fold band to inside along foldline and stitch down neatly.

BUTTONHOLE BAND

With 2¼ mm (size 13) needles and B, pick up and k 211 sts from bottom edge of welt up to beg of neckband (do not include side edge of neckband itself).

Rows 1–9 beg with a p row. Work 1 block of bricks (see rows 85–93, chart 1), beg and end each row with 1 st in B. Then make buttonholes.

Row 10 in B, k6, *cast off 7, k25 (including st already on needle); rep from * to last 13 sts, cast off 7, k6 (buttonholes will fall in centre of alternate bricks).

Row 11 p, casting on 7 sts over the 7 buttonholes.

Rows 12–20 work 1 more complete block of bricks (see rows 87–95, chart 1).

Rows 21 k (to make foldline).

Rows 22–30 work in B in k1 p1 rib.

Rows 31 and 32 as rows 10 and 11, but working in k1 p1 rib.

Rows 33–41 work in k1 p1 rib, then cast off loosely in rib.

Fold band to inside along foldline and stitch down neatly.

Neaten around buttonholes using a small buttonhole st.

BUTTONBAND

With right side facing and 2¼ mm (size 13) needles and B, pick up and k 211 sts from bottom of neckband (do not include side edge of neckband itself) to bottom edge of welt (right side facing).

Rows 1–20 work 2 complete blocks of bricks (see rows 85–95, chart 1), beg and end each row with 1 st in B.

Row 21 k (to make foldline).

Rows 22–41 work in B in k1 p1 rib, then cast off loosely in rib. Fold band to inside along foldline and stitch down neatly. Sew on buttons.

ARMHOLE BANDS

With 3¼ mm (size 10) circular needle and B, pick up and k 176 sts around top of sleeve (right side facing).

Rounds 1–11 work 1 complete block of bricks (see rows 85–95, chart 1), beg and end with 2 rows in B, working 1 st in B between each brick. Leave sts on needle.

Important make sure that the right sleeve is put in the right armhole and the left sleeve in the left armhole. Position sleeve inside armhole (right sides together) and graft (see page 155) tog. Rep for second sleeve.

Cast on edge of right front

Odd-numbered rows are knit, worked from right to left.
Even-numbered rows are purl, worked from left to right.

Right back

Armhole

Armhole

Back of neck

CHART 3

Left back

Back of neck

CHART 4

Left front

Cast off edge

Armhole

Armhole

CHART 5

Cast off edge

Top edge

Bottom edge

Cast on edge

GLOSSARY OF KNITTING TERMS AND TECHNIQUES

As an avid knitter myself, I know how exciting it is to have a new pattern and a bag of pure wool, all wonderful colours! It is a very great temptation to begin knitting without paying heed to the preliminary instructions and helpful hints. All too often, though, this results in disappointment, even disaster. To help you avoid such disappointment, listed below are a number of hints and methods that, if used, will result in a sweater you can be proud of.

NEEDLES

In Great Britain, knitting needles used to be sized by number – the higher the number, the smaller the needle. Now, metric sizing has been adopted and the smaller the metric size, the smaller the needle. In the book metric sizes are given with English sizes in brackets.

Knitting needle sizes used in the book

Metric	English
2¼ mm	13
3¼ mm	10
4 mm	8
4½ mm	7
5 mm	6

USING CIRCULAR NEEDLES

These are available in a variety of lengths so, when buying a circular needle for a pattern in the book, look under 'Materials' to see which length of needle you need.

Sweaters worked in the round are attractive because there are no seams, which results in a smoother line and, consequently, a better fit. Here are some tips for using a circular needle successfully.

● When working the first round after casting on, make sure the stitches are not twisted round the needle before you knit the first stitch.

● All rounds are knit (unless otherwise stated).

● Loop a short strand of brightly coloured wool around the first stitch of each round so that you can find the beginning easily.

● You can knit from circular needles lengthways instead of conventional needles when you have a great number of stitches.

● When working in **rows** with a circular needle, when you have worked a row, simply turn the work round and use the right-hand tip of the needle to work along the row in the opposite direction.

USING A SET OF 4 DOUBLE-POINTED NEEDLES

When you are using a set of 4 double-pointed needles for working cuffs, for example, divide the number to be cast on evenly between 3 of the needles. Using the fourth needle, work all the stitches on the first needle so that they are then on the fourth needle. The first needle is now free. Use this needle to work all the stitches on the second needle and then use this needle to complete the round, working all the stitches on the fourth needle. Work each successive round in this way.

CASTING ON

There are several ways of casting on, but the one used throughout the book, which produces a very neat edge, is known as the cable method. You need 2 needles, then:

● make a slip knot and place it on the left-hand needle
● insert the right-hand needle through the slip knot and knit it and slip new stitch onto left-hand needle.
● insert the right-hand needle between the 2 stitches on the left-hand needle, wind the wool around the tip of the right-hand needle, draw the loop you've made through between the stitches and then slip it onto the left-hand needle.
● Repeat this last step until you have cast on the required number of stitches.

CASTING OFF

Make sure you always cast off in pattern, that is, cast off knit stitches knitwise and purl stitches purlwise unless otherwise stated.

CASTING OFF KNITWISE

● Knit the first 2 stitches.
● With the left-hand needle, lift the first stitch over the second stitch and drop it off the needle.
● Knit the next stitch and repeat the second step and so on until you have cast off the required number of stitches.

CASTING OFF PURLWISE

● Purl the first 2 stitches.
● With the left-hand needle, lift the first stitch over the second stitch and drop it off the needle.
● Purl the next stitch and repeat the second step and so on until you have cast off the required number of stiches.

TENSION

This is *the* most important thing to get right if the finished sweater is to be a success – if the tension is not correct, the result can be disastrous. This is because the tension determines the shape and size of the sweater so any variation, no matter how small, will alter the look of the finished garment. It is, therefore, important that the tension given at the beginning of each pattern is matched before you start to knit. The size of needle given for each pattern is my own choice, but you may need to use a different size of needle to achieve the correct result.

To find out if you need to use a different size of needle, work a tension square. This may seem to be a nuisance and a waste of time, but it will save you the aggravation of a finished sweater that is the wrong size and shape.

Knit the square in pattern or stocking stitch as directed, casting on about 10 more stitches and working about 10 more rows than the number of stitches or rows to 10 cm (4 in). Lay the finished square on a flat surface and, using a metal tape measure or plastic ruler, count the number of stitches to 10 cm (4 in) one way and the number of rows to 10 cm (4 in) the other, measuring over the centre of the square.

● If there are too *many* stitches to 10 cm (4 in), work another tension square with *larger* needles.

● If there are too *few* stitches to 10 cm (4 in) try again with *smaller* needles. (It is the tension that is important, not the needle size.)

Once you have achieved the correct tension you can rest safe in the knowledge that your finished sweater will work out exactly like the pattern.

USING CHARTS

Every pattern in this book uses a chart. On the chart, each square represents a stitch and each line of squares represents a row of knitting.

When working from a chart using 2 needles, the knit rows are worked from right to left and the purl rows from left to right. The colours given on the chart correspond to the sweaters in the photographs, but you can, of course, use any colours you like instead. If you do use different colours, it will be easiest if you copy the chart onto graph paper substituting your own colours, but take care to copy it *exactly*, stitch for stitch.

When working from a chart, start at stitch 1, row 1, unless the instructions specify otherwise.

FAIR ISLE KNITTING

When you are using 2 or more different colours of wool

at any one time, carry the yarns not in use across the back of the work, twisting them with the wool in use before you knit the next stitch every 1 to 2 stitches, remembering to stretch the stitches to their correct width to keep them elastic and never pull the floating strands too tight. This will keep your knitting tidy and avoid holes forming.

INCREASING

TO INCREASE IN A KNIT STITCH
● Knit into the front of the stitch but do not slip it off the needle.
● Knit into the back of the same stitch, dropping it off the needle.

TO INCREASE IN A PURL STITCH
● Work as given for knit stitches above but work purlwise.

DECREASING

TO DECREASE KNITWISE
● Pass the tip of the right-hand needle into the second stitch on the left-hand needle, then into the first stitch.
● Knit these 2 stitches together, making 1 stitch.

TO DECREASE PURLWISE
● Pass the tip of the right-hand needle into the front of the first and second stitches on the left-hand needle.
● Purl the 2 stitches together.

TO DECREASE MORE THAN 1 STITCH
Cast off the required number of stitches using the casting off method given above.

PICKING UP STITCHES

It is not difficult to achieve a really professional finish when picking up stitches for buttonhole bands or around neck edges as long as you remember the following:
● measure the edge you are picking up stitches along and mark each couple of centimetres (inch) with a pin, divide the number of stitches to be picked up by the measurement and then pick up that number of stitches between each pair of pins.
● never work too close to the edge: put the tip of the

needle through the work 2 strands down (right side facing) from the edge (if you work too near the edge, the result will be uneven).

HOW TO PICK UP A STITCH
● Insert the tip of the right-hand needle through the work from the right side, wind the wool around the needle and then draw a loop through to the right side – as if you were knitting a stitch.
● Transfer the loop to the left-hand needle and knit it. (Work into small stitches rather than loose loops wherever possible.)

BLOCKING

This is another important factor in the making of a well-finished sweater. Blocking each piece of knitting once it has been worked is much easier and gives a far better finish than blocking the finished sweater. This is how it is done.
● Turn work to wrong side and pin it to an ironing board, easing it into shape and the required measurements.
● Cover it with a damp cloth and press it lightly with a hot iron, making sure that you do not move the iron to and fro, but press, lift it up and then press again evenly over the work, omitting any ribbing. (You will fit a sleeve onto your ironing board most of the time, but when you are blocking the front and back of a sweater, pin the shoulder at the top of the board and then smooth it down the length of the board until it is the required length minus the welt, press, then repeat for the next ironing-board width of work and so on. Alternatively, lay a doubled blanket or two large towels on the floor or a large table, pin the front and back of the sweater out to the required measurements and then press.)
   It is also very important to keep the work as neat as possible at the back, so weave in all loose ends using a darning needle – never just cut off the loose ends and leave them as even tight knots come undone and the knitting unravels.

POCKET LININGS

Pockets *can* make a sweater look beautifully finished, but if attention is not paid to the detail of them, they can equally completely spoil it so, when you sew in a pocket lining, remember the following:

● never sew in a pocket lining until the sweater has been blocked and pressed
● pin all the edges of the lining that are to be stitched in place and tack the opening down
● slip stitch the pocket in place by lifting a loop from the edge of the lining and a loop from the back of the main body of work (not a strand that has been carried along at the back) and lift next loop above it for next slip stitch as stitches sewn out of line will prevent the sweater hanging perfectly.

GRAFTING

This is a means of joining 2 knitted edges together without the bulk that results from casting off and then sewing the edges together. It gives a very smooth appearance so shoulder seams, particularly, look better grafted. Grafting is usually worked before the knitting is removed from the needles, but you will also find in the patterns that you are asked to graft a seam between 2 stitch holders or a needle and a stitch holder or a needle and a cast on edge.
   There are 3 methods of grafting, as follows:

METHOD 1
● Take the 2 pieces of knitting to be joined together, with the stitches still on the needles, placing the needles parallel to each other with right sides of both pieces together.
● Take a third needle in your right hand, pass its tip through the first stitch on both needles and knit them together as one stitch.
● Repeat the second step for the second stitch and then lift the first stitch over the second stitch and off the right-hand needle just like when you cast off. Continue in this way until all the stitches have been cast off.

METHOD 2
● Thread a darning needle with a length of the same colour wool as the edges you want to join together.
● Abut the edges of the 2 pieces of knitting to be joined together on a flat surface (right sides up).
● Pass the darning needle knitwise through the first stitch on the front needle and slip the stitch off the knitting needle.
● Pass the darning needle purlwise through the second stitch on the same needle, leaving the stitch on the needle.

• Pass the darning needle purlwise through the first stitch on the back needle and slip the stitch off the knitting needle.

• Pass the darning needle knitwise through the second stitch on the back needle, leaving the stitch on the knitting needle.

• Rep this process, from the third step above, until all the stitches have been joined together, then pull the strand of wool so as to form stitches of the same size as the knitted ones (holding the other end at the beginning of the row) and finish off by darning in the loose ends at the back of the piece of knitting.

METHOD 3

Joining sleeve seams

• Slip the stitches left on the needle onto a double-pointed needle.

• With right sides together, place the stitches on the double-pointed needle against the cast on edge.

• Using one of a pair of needles, insert the tip through the 1st stitch on the double-pointed needle and then through the 1st stitch of the row of knitting below the cast on edge.

• Wind the wool around the needle and draw a loop through both stitches, as if knitting a stitch.

• Repeat with the 2nd stitch on the double-pointed needle and the 2nd stitch on the cast on edge, so that there are 2 stitches on the right-hand needle.

• Using the double-pointed needle, lift the 1st stitch over the 2nd stitch and drop it off (as in casting off).

• Repeat until the end of the row has been reached and all the stitches cast off.

Inserting a sleeve

• Slip the stitches left on the needle onto a circular needle.

• With the right sides together, insert the sleeve into the armhole and work as for joining sleeve seams (above).

RIBBING

The ribbing for the buttonbands, cuffs, welts and so on of some of the garments in the book are of double thickness. This gives a smarter finish and results in a more professional look. When the ribbing is double thickness, a ridge is worked halfway through. This is referred to in all the patterns as the foldline and this

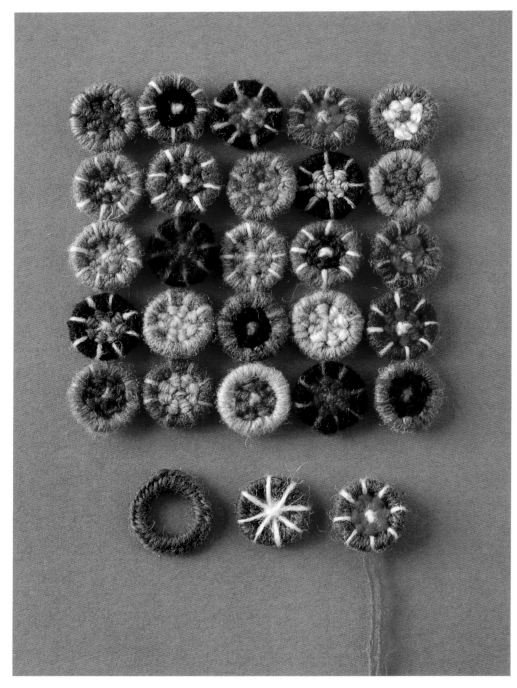

foldline must always be on the outside of the finished garment. The ribbing is then stitched neatly into place on the wrong side.

BUTTONHOLES

Good buttonholes are an important part of the finished sweater and so it is well worth giving them some close attention. Instructions for making the buttonholes are given in each pattern, but it is essential to reinforce them when the garment is finished otherwise they will not hold together, be easy to use or provide a professional finish.

One of the best ways to reinforce buttonholes is the following method. On either vertical or horizontal buttonholes, work neat buttonhole stitches along each side. The stitches should be almost touching and of an even size, but they should not be squashed too closely together as this will stretch the buttonhole out of shape. At either end of the buttonhole, as you come to them, work 3 straight stitches.

PLEATS

The sleeves of some of the garments have pleats and these are made before the sleeves are put into the armholes. Be sure to make the folds as instructed. Pin them first so that you can check that they are each of equal size and evenly spaced and only then stitch them in place, stitching through all 3 thicknesses of the pleat.

FRILLS

At first sight the frills look a daunting prospect, but if you follow the instructions step by step, they are not difficult at all and will give you a great sense of pride and satisfaction when you have finished the sweater. Bear the following in mind:
● make sure that the frills are turned down onto the right side of the work before you start a new frill
● pick up the stitches for each new frill along the rows indicated by the markers
● when you are working frills along the neck edge and at the wrists, pick up the stitches on the inside of the work.

DORSET CROSSWHEEL BUTTONS

These handmade buttons have been used on all the cardigans in the book and add a special touch to the finished sweater. Use the main colour for the edge and highlight colours to work the centre – you will be surprised how easy these buttons are to make.

MATERIALS

Plastic or brass curtain rings to fit buttonholes
Darning needle
Strands of yarn in 3 colours (A, B, C)

INSTRUCTIONS

Hold the ring and tie the strand of A to it. Thread the darning needle with the other end and work buttonhole stitch all round the ring, joining the wool to the first stitch and completely covering the ring with the knot of the stitches on the inside. Join the strand of B to the ring and work 8 spokes by winding the strand round the ring so that each spoke consists of a front and a back strand, twisting in the centre, keeping the spokes equal distances apart. Wind firmly but not too tightly and finish by working a firm cross stitch in the centre that holds all the strands together. Weave in the loose ends. Join on the strand of C at the back of the centre of the button and bring it through to the front. Backstitch in a clockwise fashion, back over one spoke, then pass the needle under the next spoke, backstitch over that and so on to produce a spider's web pattern. Leave a tiny gap between the edge of the backstitching and the buttonhole edge and weave in the ends.

CROCHET

CHAIN STITCH

● Make a slip knot and insert the hook.
● With the wool looped over your index finger, push the hook through the first knot and catch it on the yarn. Pull the yarn through the first knot to form a new loop on hook.
● Repeat until you have the required number of chains.

DOUBLE CROCHET

● Insert the hook into the 2nd chain from the hook, with the yarn around the hook draw through a loop, place the yarn around the hook, draw through 2 loops.

HALF TREBLE

● Yarn around the hook, then insert the hook into the 3rd chain from the hook, with the yarn around the hook draw a loop, place the yarn around the hook, draw through 3 loops.

TREBLE

● Yarn around the hook, then insert the hook into the 4th chain from the hook, with the yarn around the hook draw through a loop, place the yarn around the hook and draw through 2 loops, place the yarn around the hook and draw through last 2 loops.

CHAIN STITCH (EMBROIDERY)

● Bring the needle out on the centreline. Insert the needle back in the same point and, with the thread *under* the tip of the needle, bring the needle out again at a point slightly below. Continue to make stitches by inserting the needle at the point where the thread emerges.

STOCKISTS

There are bound to be some people who don't have the time or space to attempt natural dyeing, but who would love to knit these patterns using naturally dyed yarns. Complete kits for all the patterns are available, as are 115 g (4 oz) balls of the individual colours for those who have difficulty with dyeing a particular shade. For either a kit or yarn please send an SAE for the current price list to:
The Natural Dye Company
Stanbridge
Wimborne
Dorset BH21 4JD, England
Tel: (0258) 840549

The wool used in the book is 9 count Cheviot singles unbleached (knits as a 4 ply).
Similar wool can be obtained from:
Craftsman's Mark Ltd.
Tone Dale Mill
Wellington
Somerset TA21 0AW, England
Tel: (0823) 667266
(Quote wool reference 8's medium-weight yarn.)

Rowan Yarns
Green Lane Mill
Holmfirth
West Yorkshire HD7 1RW, England
Tel: (0484) 681881
(Quote wool reference 201 light tweed scoured)

Texere
College Mill
Barkerend Road
Bradford
West Yorkshire BD3 9AQ, England
Tel: (0274) 722191

Rowan Yarns do a good selection of yarns and colours in a 4 ply wool. These are readily available from most good wool shops worldwide, but are not naturally dyed.

Dyestuffs, equipment and mordants can be obtained from:
Ashill Colour Studio
Clovers
Church Street
Alcombe
Minehead
Somerset TA24 6BL, England
Tel: (0643) 702449

Fibrecrafts
Style Cottage
Lower Eashing
Godalming
Surrey GU7 2QD, England
Tel: (04868) 21853

Fibrecrafts
Elterwater
Cumbria, England
Tel: (09667) 346

Fibrecrafts
Cider Press Centre
Dartington
Totnes
Devon TQ9 6JE, England
Tel: (0803) 864171

The mordant Oxalic Acid is only available from a pharmaceutical chemist, and other mordants can be purchased there too.

2 cm (¾ in) brass button rings can be bought from:
Frank Herring and Sons
27 High West Street
Dorchester
Dorset DT1 1UP, England
Tel: (0305) 67917